entertain
epicurean

stylish seasonal dishes to
share with friends

Catherine Bell

Photography by
Keiran Scott

TANDEM PRESS

First published in 2000 by
TANDEM PRESS
2 Rugby Road
Birkenhead
Auckland 10
NEW ZEALAND
Reprinted 2001
Copyright © 2000 Catherine Bell

ISBN 1 877178 65 9

Cover and text design by Christine Hansen
Produced by *BookNZ*, Auckland
Printed in Hong Kong by
Everbest Printing Co. Ltd.

The recipes contained within this book have been collected over a number of years from a wide variety of sources. Regrettably, records of these sources were not always kept. I apologise to anyone who may feel they have not been adequately acknowledged.

contents

preface

The Epicurean is much more than a cooking school. It doesn't just teach people to cook. It inspires and excites them about food. It makes them think about what is good food and how to make it an enjoyable part of their life, both in the kitchen and at the table.

Each time we hold a cooking class at the Epicurean we are celebrating all that is good about food, not just it's preparation but the enjoyment of eating it also.

One of the ways we do this of course, is by inviting chefs from home and abroad to teach. Whereas in the early days, our classes were a platform on which chefs showcased their restaurants, today our guest chefs are, more often than not, invited to teach at the Epicurean on the basis of their ability to relate to the cook at home and are asked to present dishes that are easily prepared with the usual equipment found in most kitchens. Not everyone has the range of skills, the knowledge or simply the time to create haute cuisine at home and although all these things are attainable, most of us lean towards lighter, fresher and certainly faster meals that look and taste great. However this does not deter our guests from introducing their audience to new ingredients or methods.

There are bonuses for me too. I consider myself very fortunate to have had the opportunity to work alongside and get to know some of New Zealand's and Australia's finest chefs as well as several from other countries around the world. I may not be able to sit in class and watch them at work but it is equally inspiring to spend time with these people, to 'talk' food, to eat out at restaurants, visit markets or other places of culinary interest, and to assist them as they teach.

I am constantly impressed and awed by New Zealand's own chefs. It is no wonder so many of our chefs do well overseas. Our chefs are amongst a very few in the world who are not bound by culture or tradition and who seem to have a natural talent that sees them taking the best from all cuisines to interpret and mould them into dishes that fit with the New Zealand lifestyle and palate.

This book allows me to share with you a collection of the best dishes cooked at the Epicurean by myself and our guest chefs, both local and international, since its inception 11 years ago.

The chosen theme of 'entertaining' does not however mean food that takes hours to prepare or that requires a raft of expensive ingredients. I have been careful, as in my first book, *Everyday Epicurean*, to select dishes for their simplicity and/or ease of preparation. Formal entertaining is almost a thing of the past, although classes on more elegant dining are as popular as ever. On the whole though, I think people find it much more fun to put a fabulous platter in the middle of the table and ask their guests to help themselves! You'll find a little bit of both in the pages that follow.

acknowledgements

1999 was an extraordinary year in the life of the Epicurean. As we moved locations, doubled in size as a result, won TopShop, launched our website and my first book, *Everyday Epicurean*, I depended on many, many people for many, many things along the way, and received an enormous amount of support, encouragement and confidence from them all.

My children, Tom and Olivia. I promised them more time and in fact was there for them even less. One day …

My father, Bill, who is always there for me when I need to off-load; and to all my family for their on-going support.

Jacqueline Walker and Claire Aldous who, between them, keep the cookschool running like a well-oiled machine, for their brilliance with food and their sheer hard work. This book is a testament to them, from recipe development, testing and preparation for photography, I couldn't have done any of it without them.

All my staff at Epicurean, both in the school, cookstore and espresso bar, who keep everything running smoothly and who give their very best at every moment.

Our customers who continue to support both the Epicurean and me personnally.

To the many cooks and chefs who have taught classes at Epicurean over the last eleven years and to those whose recipes have contributed to this book, especially Ray McVinnie. Ray has taught so many classes he is almost a permanent member of staff.

Kieran Scott, whose photography once again enhances these pages. What talent!

The publishing team at Tandem Press: Bob Ross and Helen Benton, Sara Haddad, Jane Hingston, Alison Mudford and Christine Hansen. True professionals, all of them.

Catherine Bell (centre) with Claire Aldous (left) and Jacqueline Walker (right).

introduction

Everyone loves to entertain friends at home. Whether it's something you do every week, or only once a year, and whether you do it casually or go all out, it should be an enjoyable experience, not just for your guests but for you also. *Entertaining Epicurean* is intended to make entertaining both fun and enjoyable, with recipes that do not require hours of preparation or great forethought.

In it you'll see that the chapters are themed according to the style of dining or food, for example Al Fresco, Asian Feast or Barbecue. The dishes within each of these chapters are a collection, rather than a menu, gathered from many of the classes held at Epicurean over the last few years. So, whereas you will find it easy to plan a menu from just one of these collections, many of the dishes will happily cross-pollinate.

Many of the dishes are versatile enough to be used in several ways, for instance the Spicy Chicken and Onion Tart on page 22 is perfect as a brunch dish, but could just as easily be made into tiny individual tarts for an hors d'oeuvres, or served for dinner with a salad.

In the same way, many dishes can be served casually, from a platter, or be plated individually for more formal presentation. If you want to make life easier, choose the platter!

Most of the ingredients used will be familiar to you. If not, you will find a reference to them in the head note or in the glossary which begins on page 194. If an ingredient proves hard to locate there is very often an alternative so don't let it put you off trying a particular dish.

Above all, I hope that everyone who reads this book will want, as a result, to get in the kitchen and cook. It's what we do in all our classes, inspire and enthuse both about cooking and the end result – eating round a table with people we care about.

Have fun!

the basic kitchen

In addition to the usual pots, pans, bowls and utensils, there are many gadgets and pieces of equipment that will make cooking far more efficient and enjoyable. When buying major pieces of equipment such as saucepans, knives or a food processor, I advise you to do your homework first, then purchase the best you can afford.

Listed below are the essentials any cook needs to produce a wide range of dishes. It may seem a long list, but these things can be acquired gradually as the need arises. You may be surprised just how many you have already.

Pot & Pans
3 x saucepans, 14 cm, 16 cm & 18 cm
  (5½", 6½", 7")
1 x 20 cm (8") saucepan, either with one long
  handle or two handles
1 x stockpot, 8-10 litres (16-20 pints)
2 x frying pans, 24 cm & 28 cm (9½" x 11")
1 x roasting pan & rack
1 x ovenproof casserole

Utensils
Set of four mixing bowls
Measuring spoons
Measuring cups, ¼, ⅓, ½ & 1 cup
Measuring jug, 1 litre (2 pint) capacity with
  graduated markings
Meat thermometer
Metal utensils – fish slice, slotted spoon, fork, large
  spoon, ladle, potato masher
Four-sided grater
Wire whisk
Bottle opener
Can opener
Corkscrew
Lemon squeezer

2-3 wooden spoons
2 x rubber spatulas, preferably heat resistant
Colander
2 x wire-mesh sieves, large & small
Egg beater
Tongs
Vegetable peeler
Pepper grinder
Chopping board
Garlic press

Knives
10 cm (4") paring knife
15 cm (6") utility knife
20-23 cm (8-10") cook's knife
Bread knife
Sharpening steel

Baking Equipment
Baking sheets
Rolling pin
Cooling rack
Pastry brush
Teflon sheet
Variety of baking tins for cakes, muffins, tarts, loaves

Electrical Equipment
Set of scales, with metric and imperial readings
Hand blender or cake mixer
Food processor

Optional extras – things I wouldn't be without
Benriner slicer – a very sharp Japanese slicer,
  adjustable and with three julienne blades.
Electric spice grinder – an inexpensive electric coffee
  grinder dedicated to the job.
Zester – a simple tool that strips the zest from citrus
  fruit.
Ridged cast-iron grill – for chargrilling indoors –
  available in many sizes and shapes.
Bamix food machine – a wand mixer – blends soup
  in the saucepan.
Pressure cooker – long-cooked casseroles and soups

or freshly cooked beans can be achieved in a fraction of the time.

Ice-cream machine – small, relatively inexpensive machines to make smooth, creamy ice-creams, sorbets, frozen yoghurts.

Pasta machine – a hand-rolling machine that clamps to the bench.

Salad spinner – dries salad leaves easily and efficiently.

Simmer mat – if you cook on gas, one of these will enable you to cook at a really low heat.

Wok – no kitchen should be without one. Essential for Asian stirfries, steaming, deep frying.

Stainless steel dough scraper – for scooping up chopped vegetables or herbs.

Bamboo steamer with two layers – can be used to steam anything.

Candy thermometer – use for deep frying and preserving.

Spraypump olive oil mister – gives a fine spray of your chosen olive oil, saves using a pastry brush to oil vegetables, meat or grill pans.

Garlic peeler – a flexible tube that peels garlic with one roll under the hand.

Kitchen torch – a refillable gas flame to caramelise the tops of crème brûlée and other sweet dishes.

Mesh food hoods – use outdoors to protect food from insects.

the entertainers kitchen

Entertaining at home does not mean you need a kitchen that any caterer would be proud of. Most cooks can produce a meal for six or eight people with relative ease, using what equipment they already have on hand. It is only usually when numbers increase that it can put a strain on both equipment and facilities. It helps to plan a menu around what you have and then

borrow or hire anything extra. However if entertaining is a frequent occurance it might pay to have more than one of some things e.g. 12 ramekins instead of 6, 2 x 24 cm tart tins etc.

- Maximise fridge space by
  - using rectangular take-away food containers with plastic lids which stack on top of each other. These are great for sauces, chopped vegetables and herbs.
  - use zip-lock plastic bags to store vegetables and salad greens prior to assembly
  - use plastic trays (rather than odd shaped platters and bowls) to store foods before and after cooking.
- Create more bench space by setting up a trestle table nearby.
- Buy a caterers roll of extra wide plastic wrap.
- Collect a few large trays, platters and bowls – these can be used for cocktail food, on buffets and for casual help-yourself dinners round the table.

credits

I would like to thank the following companies for allowing me to use their products in the photographs within this book.

Acland Holdings

Country Road Homewares

Domestic Agencies

Freedom Furniture

La Cigale

Linens and More

Maytime Marketing

Nest

The Studio of Tableware

brunch

This is the late breakfast or early lunch that has real social connotations. Even before the recent arrival of our café culture, brunch was seen as a rather luxurious way to spend a Sunday morning that then stretched on into the afternoon. For some it is still a treat, but for others it has become a weekend ritual, a time to catch up with friends and to really relax. The food is hearty, a chance to enjoy a full cooked breakfast with all the trimmings that there is never time for on a working day. But there is more to brunch than bacon and eggs. It's a popular topic for 'Gourmet on the Run', the result being rather an interesting collection of dishes.

sourdough pancakes with grilled nectarines and runny honey

Pancakes have been a tradition in our family, especially on holidays or special days. For years we've always served them with crispy bacon and maple syrup, but this version is also becoming a firm favourite when stone fruits are in season. It's also a chance to use one of our exceptional local honeys, such as blue borage or thistle. This batter benefits from being made the night before so it's well worth a little bit of forward thinking. Save the pan juices from the nectarines and serve alongside.

the night before

combine the yeast and water and leave for 10 minutes. Whisk in the milk and melted butter.

In another bowl mix the flour and sugar, then whisk in the yeast mixture. Cover the bowl with plastic wrap and leave in a warm place for 1 hour. The mixture should increase in volume and become bubbly. Stir down gently, cover and leave overnight at room temperature.

Just before using, stir down once more and whisk in the eggs and salt.

Preheat the grill.

Place a dot of butter in the hollow of each nectarine. Combine the honey and lemon juice and drizzle over the fruit. Place under the grill and cook until the honey is bubbling and the nectarines are beginning to turn golden.

Heat a crepe pan to medium-high and brush with a little butter. Pour or ladle on a little batter and, using a spatula, spread to about a 12 cm (5") diameter. Cook until some of the bubbles have popped and the bottom is lightly browned. Flip, brown the other side, then keep warm in a low oven until all the pancakes have been cooked.

Serve the pancakes topped with the nectarines and a further drizzle of honey.

SERVES 6

2$\frac{1}{2}$ teaspoons active dried yeast
$\frac{1}{2}$ cup (125 ml) lukewarm water
1$\frac{1}{2}$ cups (375 ml) lukewarm milk
3 tablespoons unsalted butter, melted
2 cups (260 g) plain flour
3 tablespoons sugar
2 eggs, lightly beaten
1 teaspoon salt
butter for the pan

NECTARINES
6 nectarines, halved and stoned
2 tablespoons butter
180 ml (6$\frac{1}{2}$ oz) runny honey – blue borage, thistle
juice of 3 lemons

grilled bananas with citrus and spices

You could serve the sourdough pancakes on page 12 with these bananas. Otherwise, serve them over waffles or toasted brioche or with crispy bacon. They are pretty good with ice-cream too, as a quick and easy dessert on a busy weeknight.

preheat the grill in the oven.

Peel the bananas and cut them in half lengthways. Put them, cut-side up, in a shallow oven-proof dish.

Combine the juices and spoon them over the bananas. Mix the spices with the butter and dot over the fruit.

Place the bananas under the grill and cook until golden and tender – about 6 minutes. Pull the dish out from under the grill, sprinkle with icing sugar and flaked almonds. Put back under the grill until the almonds are brown. Serve warm.

SERVES 4

4 large, firm bananas
juice of 1 lime
50 ml (2 fl oz) orange juice
pinch of ground nutmeg
pinch ground coriander
40 g (1½ oz) unsalted butter
icing sugar
2 tablespoons flaked almonds

tipsy french toast

Breakfast will never be the same again once you've introduced the family to this French toast. It's certainly the best I've ever eaten. By all means leave the alcohol out if you wish, although they won't be tipsy if you do. Simply replace it with more cream.

beat the eggs and cream together. Add the Triple Sec, sugar, zest and cinnamon and whisk to combine. Pour into a shallow dish.

Dip each croissant in the egg mixture, turning to coat. Melt a few tablespoons of butter in a frying pan and add as many croissants as will fit. Fry until golden on both sides.

Sift icing sugar over the croissants and serve straight away.

SERVES 6

5 eggs
¾ cup cream
⅓ cup Triple Sec or Grand Marnier
2 tablespoons caster sugar
zest of 1 orange
2 teaspoons cinnamon
6 plain stale croissants
6 tablespoons unsalted butter
icing sugar

baked apples on croutes

Apart from being an excellent way to use up stale bread, this is a most delicious way to prepare apples. Ray McVinnie included this in a class entitled 'Cuisine Grandmere – French Bistro fare at its best'. Choose an apple that will 'melt' as it cooks, rather than one that goes 'fluffy'.

preheat the oven to 160°C/310°F.

Spread the slices of bread thickly with butter. Peel and slice the apples and place as many as can fit on top of each slice. Brush the apples with a little melted butter and sprinkle well with sugar before placing on a buttered or lined baking tray.

Bake for 40 minutes until the bread is crisp and the apples soft and golden.

Serve with a spoonful of prunes and creme fraiche.

SERVES 6

6 x 2 cm (³/₄") thick slices of day old French bread
butter
3 cooking apples, such as Braeburn
sugar
creme fraiche and prune compote to serve

prune compote

combine all the ingredients in a saucepan and bring to the boil. Reduce the heat and simmer gently until the prunes are soft and plump, but not disintegrating – about 5–10 minutes.

Remove from the heat, cool and set aside.

MAKES 2¹/₂ CUPS

2¹/₂ cups pitted prunes
1¹/₂ cups (375 ml) red wine
¹/₂ cup (125 ml) water
zest of 1 orange
¹/₂ cup sugar
1 vanilla bean

goats cheese soufflés

Individual soufflés like these are an unusual and slightly different way to serve eggs at brunch. The goats cheese imparts an irresistible flavour. When we cooked these in 'Gourmet on the Run', several people who professed not to like goats cheese declared them delicious. As with all soufflés they are best eaten straight from the oven. However, if you wish to prepare ahead, make the mixture up to the stage where you would add the beaten egg whites, refrigerate and then warm gently when ready to proceed.

preheat the oven to 180°C/350°F.

Generously butter 6 x 185 ml (¾ cup) custard cups or ramekins and coat with cornmeal, making sure the entire surface is covered.

Melt the butter over a medium heat and add the flour. Cook for 1 minute, stirring constantly. Remove from the heat and add the milk, beating until smooth.

Return to the heat and bring slowly to the boil. The mixture will be very thick. Transfer to a large bowl and add the cheese, mixing until it has melted. Beat in the egg yolks, garlic, thyme, salt and pepper.

Beat together the egg whites and cream of tartar until stiff but not dry. Fold about one quarter of the beaten egg whites into the cheese mixture to lighten it, then fold in the rest.

Spoon the mixture into the custard cups and place them in a roasting pan. Pour enough boiling water around the cups so it comes halfway up the sides.

Cook for about 45 minutes or until the soufflés are firm and the tops nicely browned.

Serve with roasted red capsicums (see page 196) – peeled and thinly sliced, a mixed green leaf salad and walnut bread.

MAKES 6

45 g (2½ tablespoons) unsalted butter, plus extra for greasing

¾ cup cornmeal or polenta

¼ cup plain flour

⅔ cup milk

300 g (10½ oz) soft goats cheese

4 large egg yolks

2 cloves garlic, crushed

1 tablespoon fresh thyme, finely chopped

½ teaspoon sea salt

¼ teaspoon freshly ground white pepper

5 large egg whites

¼ teaspoon cream of tartar

creamed eggs with ciabatta toast

Everyone has their own special method for scrambling eggs. Certainly the subject always causes healthy debate each time it's raised here at Epicurean. The amazing results with these creamed eggs are due in part to the cooking over a bain marie and also to the addition of the cream.

in a large bowl, beat the eggs well to combine the yolks and whites, then add the cream and mix in. Melt the butter in the top of a double boiler over a gentle heat. A simple double boiler (bain marie) can be created from a ceramic or pyrex bowl set over a pan of simmering water.

Add the egg and cream mixture and cook slowly, stirring frequently. This is important to ensure smooth, creamy eggs. Remove from the heat when slightly underdone as they will continue cooking.

Season with salt and pepper and serve immediately with ciabatta toast and any of the following:

Smoked salmon and creme fraiche: slice the salmon and fold gently through the eggs. Top with a dollop of creme fraiche and sprinkle with chopped chives.

Pancetta and caramelised onion: finely slice onions and sauté in oil over a gentle heat until golden and beginning to caramelise. Remove from the pan and increase the heat. Add cooked, sliced sausage and cook until golden brown. Serve alongside the eggs.

Roasted red capsicum, tomato and anchovies: peel, seed and chop ripe tomatoes. Finely chop anchovies and slice capsicum. Mix all together and pile onto the sourdough toast. Serve alongside the eggs.

Oven roasted tomatoes, Parmesan and basil: slow roast whole tomatoes in the oven, allow to cool a little or completely. Fold grated or shaved Parmesan cheese through the eggs and serve with the tomatoes and plenty of freshly torn basil.

12 eggs
½ cup cream
1 tablespoon unsalted butter
sea salt
freshly ground pepper
slices of ciabatta bread for toasting

SERVES 4–6

17

tarragon omelette with goats cheese

We all love goats cheese at Epicurean. It crops up in classes frequently in many different ways. I usually use a goats feta for this particular dish. It crumbles easily and melts a little in the heat. For ease I always mix each omelette separately and serve them straight away while the centre is still creamy.

combine the eggs, water, cheese and tarragon in a large bowl. Season with salt , pepper and tabasco and set aside.

For each omelette, melt 1 tablespoon of butter together with $\frac{1}{2}$ tablespoon of olive oil in a 20 cm (8") non-stick skillet over a medium heat.

When hot, add half the egg mixture and cook for about 1 minute or until the eggs begin to set. Stir with a fork to form a thick mass.

With a spatula, fold the omelette in half and turn out onto a plate. Serve at once.

SERVES 2–3

6 large eggs
2 tablespoons water
120 g (4 oz) firm goats cheese, crumbled
1 tablespoon fresh tarragon, finely chopped
salt and freshly ground black pepper
dash of tabasco sauce
2 tablespoons unsalted butter
1 tablespoon olive oil

malaysian rice salad

Oh, how my mouth waters as I remember this dish. When we first came across its original version I thought it sounded rather odd, but the results were surprising – a sort of modern kedgeree. Use an oily fish and, if you are unable to find Thai basil, regular Mediterranean will do.

preheat the oven to 180°C/350°F.

Place the fish fillets on a baking tray and bake until just cooked. Turn the oven from bake to grill and while it is heating break the cooked fish into small pieces and place on a foil-covered baking tray. Cook under the hot grill, turning occasionally, until golden and crispy. Remove and set aside to cool.

Slice the turmeric, ginger, chilli and lime leaves into very fine strips. In a bowl mix the fish with the cooked rice, then add the sliced ingredients, the toasted coconut and fish sauce and set aside.

To make the dressing – place the coriander roots, garlic, chilli, avocado and basil leaves in a blender or food processor and process until smooth. Add the lime juice, oil and salt and process until the dressing is smooth and creamy.

Fold the dressing into the rice mixture and transfer to a serving bowl.

Serve with a few green salad leaves on the side.

SERVES 4–6

300 g (11 oz) fish fillets, such as trevally

1 teaspoon turmeric powder or 5 cm (2") piece fresh turmeric

1 cm (½") piece fresh ginger

1 small red chilli, seeds discarded

6 kaffir lime leaves

¼ cup Thai basil leaves

3 cups cooked white Jasmine Rice

½ cup coconut threads, toasted

2 tablespoons fish sauce

DRESSING

5 coriander roots, trimmed and chopped

1 clove garlic, chopped

1 small red chilli, seeds removed, chopped

½ small avocado, sliced

¼ cup Thai basil leaves, chopped

⅓ cup lime juice

¾ cup vegetable oil

1 teaspoon salt

turkey and jersey benne salad

Jersey Benne potatoes are like the first asparagus, long anticipated. But, unlike asparagus, the season is extremely short, so make the most of them while you can. Turkey breast is widely available and can easily be cooked by roasting in a hot oven. This dish is a perfect use for leftover Christmas turkey.

in a food processor combine the mustard and the ½ cup of vinegar, then add the olive oil in a steady stream. Add the garlic and season with salt and pepper. Set aside.

In a saucepan, cover the potatoes with cold water and bring to the boil. Simmer gently until tender then drain and leave to cool.

Heat a little oil in a heavy pan and sauté the bacon until crisp, then drain on paper towels.

Mix the red onion with the 2 tablespoons of vinegar and set aside.

To assemble, mix together the potatoes, bacon, parsley, turkey and drained red onion. Add the dressing, keeping back a small amount, and mix well. Add the remaining dressing to the greens and toss to combine.

Place the greens on a platter and arrange the turkey salad on top. Garnish with flatleaf parsley and serve.

SERVES 6–8

2 tablespoons Dijon mustard
½ cup white wine vinegar, plus 2 tablespoons
1 cup olive oil
1 clove garlic, crushed
sea salt
freshly ground pepper
12–16 Jersey Benne potatoes, washed
250 g (9 oz) bacon, chopped
1 small red onion, chopped
⅓ cup flatleaf parsley, coarsely chopped, extra for garnish
4 cups cooked turkey, shredded
2 bunches rocket
1 bunch watercress

spicy chicken and onion tart

The onion filling for this tart also makes a really good accompaniment to any grilled chicken, lamb or beef – it's simply a spicy onion marmalade.

It's very important not to hurry the slow cooking of these onions. If you do, by turning up the heat, you risk catching the base of the pan and burning the spices. Serve this tart with a green salad and some crusty bread.

combine the flour, salt and butter in a food processor. Process briefly until the mixture resembles breadcrumbs.

Mix the egg yolk and water together and add to the dry ingredients through the feed tube. Mix until just combined.

Tip onto the bench and bring together quickly with your hands.

Form into a flat disc, wrap in plastic film and refrigerate for 20–30 minutes.

Roll out the prepared pastry and line a 28 cm (11") tart tin. Refrigerate for 30 minutes until firm.

Preheat the oven to 200°C/400°F.

Bake blind (see glossary, page 194) for 15 minutes, remove the baking beans and bake for a further 10–15 minutes.

To make the filling, heat the oil to a medium heat in a frying pan and add the spices.

Cook for 1 minute then add the tomato paste and cook for another minute. Add the onion, garlic and ginger and cook slowly, stirring occasionally, until very soft – about 40 minutes. Take off the heat and cool.

Slice the chicken thinly and toss in the spice paste.

Spread the onion mixture over the pastry base and lay the chicken on top.

Bake in the oven for 20 minutes or until the chicken is just cooked but still succulent and the pastry is golden.

To serve, spoon dollops of sour cream and mango chutney on top of the tart and sprinkle with plenty of coriander sprigs.

SERVES 6

PASTRY
170 g (6 oz) plain flour
pinch salt
100 g (3½ oz) unsalted butter
1 egg yolk
1 tablespoon iced water

ONION FILLING
4 tablespoons vegetable oil
2 teaspoons ground cumin
2 teaspoons ground coriander
¼ teaspoon cinnamon
2 tablespoons tomato paste
4 large onions, finely sliced
3 cloves garlic, crushed
2 cm (¾") piece of ginger

CHICKEN
6 boneless, skinless chicken thighs
2 tablespoons tandoori spice paste

GARNISH
sour cream
mango chutney
coriander sprigs

mushroom and kidney on fried toast and tapenade

I grew up eating lambs kidneys and lambs fry for breakfast, especially on exam mornings, but rarely eat them now. This dish from Varick Neilson is infinitely more exotic than what my mother put in front of us, although the same two rules she always stuck to apply here as well. One, that the kidneys had to be fresh, not frozen, and two, they had to be pink in the middle so they'd be succulent and tender.

place the tapenade ingredients in the food processor and process to a coarse paste. Makes 2 cups.

Heat a little oil or butter in a large heavy sauté pan and pan-fry the kidneys over a high heat for 2–3 minutes on each side. Remove and set aside.

Place the mushrooms in the same pan – gill-side down, adding a little more olive oil or butter. Season with sea salt and pepper and cook 3 minutes each side. Return the kidneys to the pan and cook for a further 5 minutes until pink, longer if not.

Remove from the pan and allow to rest. Return the pan to the heat and pour in the sherry. Allow to reduce until syrupy.

Preheat the grill.

Brush the bread liberally with olive oil. Grill until golden on both sides.

Spread the toast liberally with tapenade. Place a mushroom on each slice and arrange 4 kidney halves on top of each one. Spoon over the pan juices.

Serve immediately.

SERVES 6

TAPENADE

75 g (3½ tablespoons) capers, drained and rinsed

50 g (about 9 large anchovies) anchovy fillets, drained

3 chillies, seeded and chopped

12 basil leaves

120 ml (4½ fl oz) olive oil

450 g (15½ oz) black olives, pitted

freshly ground white pepper

3 tablespoons finely diced sundried tomatoes,

20 cloves garlic, roasted and puréed (see page 196)

olive oil or butter for frying

12 fresh lambs kidneys, trimmed and halved

6 large field mushrooms, stalks removed

salt and freshly ground white pepper

¼ cup sherry

6 slices country bread

100 ml (3½ fl oz) olive oil

crescentina

I will always remember this bread, because the day I made this in class I lost my rings. Having taken them off to knead the bread, I never saw them again. However, this should not put you off baking this tasty version of focaccia, the famous Italian bread, we have all become so fond of in recent years. If you wish, leave the dough in the fridge overnight as this enhances the flavour significantly. It is also a good way to ensure you have freshly baked bread for the morning. Just bring the dough back to room temperature, shape it, give it a final rise and then bake.

sprinkle the yeast over $\frac{1}{4}$ cup of lukewarm water and leave to dissolve.

Put the bacon into the food processor and chop finely. Add the yeast, 1 cup of the flour, $\frac{1}{2}$ cup of the water, the salt and the sugar. Process together and, while the motor is running, add the remaining flour and water. When the dough just comes together in a ball stop the machine.

Put about 1 tablespoon of oil in a large bowl and place the dough in the bowl, turning it to coat well with the oil. Cover with plastic wrap and set aside in a warm place to rise until doubled in size – about 3 hours.

Preheat the oven to 200°C/400°F.

Oil a 20 cm (8") square baking tin. Take the risen dough, place it in the centre and, using your fingers, gently spread it out until it fills the tin. Cover with plastic wrap and leave in a warm place until it has risen almost to the top of the tin.

Brush the top with plenty of olive oil, sprinkle the top with sea salt and bake for 30 minutes or until the top is golden. Unmould onto a cooling rack. Serve while still warm.

SERVES 6–8

$1\frac{1}{4}$ teaspoons active dried yeast
$1\frac{1}{4}$ cups lukewarm water
250 g (9 oz) streaky bacon, trimmed of rind but not fat
$3\frac{1}{4}$ cups plain flour
1 teaspoon salt
pinch of sugar
extra virgin olive oil
sea salt

al fresco

Eating out of doors is one of life's simple pleasures. Some of my most memorable meals have been al fresco – Christmas lunch under the trees in the park, at a long table on an ancient terrace in Italy, picnics beside a river, lake or the sea in various spots around the world. The locations may vary but all these meals had one thing in common: good food that was seasonal, fresh and uncomplicated. In all cases, the dishes are placed on the table for people to help themselves at their leisure – a sort of continuous feast.

tomato tarts

I was inspired to make these after eating something similar at Neil Perry's Star's Restaurant (now Wokpool) in Sydney. These little morsels are quick to prepare and make the most of summer tomatoes. Larger 12 cm (5") tarts are perfect for a first course or lunch, with a few salad leaves on the side. I know I always say this but for this dish only the very sweetest tomatoes will do!

cut 5–6 cm (2–2½") circles of pastry and prick all over with a fork. Place on a baking sheet and chill in the fridge until firm. Brush with olive oil.

Preheat the oven to 220°C/425°F.

Bake the pastry rounds until almost cooked, but not yet golden on the edges.

Remove from the oven and spread lightly with Dijon mustard. Top with sliced tomatoes, alternating if using red and yellow.

Return to the oven and bake just until the tomatoes are soft and the pastry is golden and crisp. Sprinkle with finely chopped herbs, salt and pepper and serve.

1 quantity of ready rolled puff pastry sheets, 23 cm (9") square
extra virgin olive oil
Dijon mustard
red and yellow cherry tomatoes or small red tomatoes
basil or Italian parsley to garnish
salt and freshly ground pepper

variations

Instead of Dijon mustard, use basil pesto or a cream cheese or mascarpone mixed with fresh herbs and seasoned well with salt and pepper.

YIELDS 14 X 6 CM (2½") TARTS FROM ONE PASTRY SHEET

chilled tomato and couscous soup

Inspiration for dishes to teach in our classes comes from many places. This one is adapted from a recipe in Food of the Sun by Alistair Little. This dish requires little more than the chopping and combining of ingredients – perfect for a hot summer's day!

heat the vinegar and dissolve the sugar in it. Cool.

Mix together the tomatoes, passata and basil. Season with salt and pepper. Now add the vinegar mixture, a drop at a time, tasting constantly until it is to your liking. Chill.

Bring the water to the boil and pour it over a few crushed mint leaves. Remove the mint and pour the water over the couscous. Stir and add the lemon zest and juice, then mix in the prepared vegetables and parsley. Add the olive oil and mix well. Season and chill.

Put a generous spoonful of couscous in the centre of each soup plate. Ladle the tomato soup around and drizzle with yoghurt and a little olive oil. Scatter over the small basil leaves and a few extra parsley leaves.

SERVES 6

1 tablespoon white wine vinegar

2 teaspoons sugar

4 large ripe tomatoes, peeled, seeded and chopped or 1 tin (400 g/14 oz) Italian tomatoes in juice

1 litre (1¾ pints) passata (Italian puréed tomatoes)

handful basil leaves, shredded

sea salt and freshly ground pepper

300 ml (½ pint) plain, unsweetened yoghurt

small basil leaves and parsley to garnish

COUSCOUS

1 cup (250 ml) boiling water

a few mint leaves, shredded

225 g (8 oz) instant couscous

zest and juice of 2 lemons

½ red onion, chopped

1 red capsicum, chopped

1 yellow or green capsicum, chopped

1 red chilli, finely chopped

handful Italian parsley leaves, coarsely chopped

150 ml (5½ fl oz) extra virgin olive oil

carpaccio of beef with peanuts and basil

In a twist of cultures we've adapted the famous Italian raw beef dish into one that celebrates the flavours of South East Asia. Assemble this dish just before serving to ensure everything tastes as fresh as possible.

heat a heavy, cast iron pan or barbecue plate until very hot. Rub the piece of beef all over with vegetable oil and season with salt and pepper. Sear quickly on all sides in the pan until the fillet is browned. This process should only take a minute as it is important that the beef does not begin to cook inside. Allow to cool and then wrap tightly in tinfoil.

Place in the freezer and chill until very, very cold and just starting to freeze.

Chop the lemongrass very finely and place in a small food processor with the chilli and mix to a paste. Add the other ingredients and mix well.

Slice the beef very thinly and arrange on a platter so each slice slightly overlaps the next. Drizzle over the dressing and sprinkle with a few peanuts. Garnish with torn basil.

SERVES 4–6

500 g (1 lb) eye fillet of beef in one piece, trimmed of all fat and sinew
vegetable oil
sea salt and freshly ground pepper
$\frac{1}{2}$ cup peanuts, roasted, skinned and roughly chopped
$\frac{3}{4}$ cup small basil leaves

DRESSING

2 stalks lemongrass, bulb end only, leaves and outer woody layers removed
1 fresh red chilli, seeded and finely chopped
4 cloves garlic, finely chopped
3 tablespoons fish sauce
juice of 4 limes
1 teaspoon sugar
1 small red onion, thinly sliced

grilled lamb and eggplant salad with
roasted potato

This dish has lots of different components that come together in one finished dish. This way the whole meal can be served on a single platter and as people serve themselves they discover what's there. The eggplant salad resembles baba ghanoush and can also be served as a dip or spread.

combine the marinade ingredients and pour over the lamb. Allow to marinate, refrigerated, for up to 2 hours.

To make the eggplant salad: preheat the oven to 200°C/400°F.

Prick the eggplants all over with the point of a small knife and place in a shallow roasting pan. Roast, turning frequently, until soft – about 20 minutes. Remove from the oven, place in a plastic bag and set aside.

When cool, remove the skins and chop the flesh roughly. In a food processor mix the eggplant, garlic and salt, then add the olive oil in a steady stream while the motor is running. Or mix all ingredients in a bowl and whisk vigorously with a wire whisk until the mixture is smooth. Stir through the parsley.

Toss the cubed potatoes in a little olive oil and salt and roast in the hot oven, turning now and again, until golden.

Preheat a grill or barbecue.

Brush the eggplant slices with olive oil and grill or barbecue until tender and well coloured.

Drain any excess marinade from the lamb and grill or barbecue until medium rare – about 2–3 minutes each side. Allow to rest for 5–10 minutes.

Cut each loin diagonally into about 6 slices. Toss the spinach in a little olive oil and ground pepper and arrange around the outside of a platter. Place the grilled eggplant in the centre and top with the lamb. Scatter the potatoes over and dress with a large spoonful of the eggplant salad. Sprinkle with chopped parsley. Serve extra eggplant salad separately.

SERVES 4–6

MARINADE
$\frac{1}{2}$ cup olive oil
juice of a lemon
$\frac{1}{2}$ teaspoon Dijon mustard
$\frac{1}{2}$ teaspoon seeded mustard
1 tablespoon chopped coriander
sea salt and freshly ground pepper

4 lamb shortloins, trimmed of any sinew

EGGPLANT PURÉE
4 medium eggplants
4 cloves garlic, finely chopped
1 teaspoon salt
1 cup extra virgin olive oil
$\frac{1}{2}$ cup finely chopped parsley

6 waxy potatoes, washed and cut into 2 cm ($\frac{3}{4}$") cubes
olive oil
salt and freshly ground pepper
2–4 eggplants (depending on the size), sliced
500g (1 lb) baby spinach, washed and trimmed
Italian parsley

roast vegetables with tahini dressing

Kate Fay is one of New Zealand's few top female chefs. Her food is fresh and modern in its approach, with a real emphasis on flavour. This is a late summer dish to serve when you are enjoying the last of the sun without the need for umbrellas. Quantities are not vital here – you just simply roast enough vegetables for the number of people eating.

preheat the oven to 225°C/450°F.

Drizzle a little olive oil in a large roasting pan and sprinkle with sea salt and pepper. Toss the prepared vegetables to lightly coat and roast until just tender, removing them from the oven as each is ready.

Blend all the dressing ingredients together. Add the spring onions and toasted sesame seeds.

Toss the vegetables in the tahini dressing and serve warm or cold.

YIELDS 3½ CUPS TAHINI DRESSING

olive oil
sea salt and freshly ground pepper
small red onions, quartered
kumara, peeled and sliced thickly
pumpkin, cut into chunks
red capsicums, seeded and cut into large pieces
button mushrooms, cleaned and stalks trimmed
small eggplants, halved lengthways
small round green beans, trimmed
snow peas
broccoli florets

TAHINI DRESSING
500 ml (2 cups) sunflower oil
200 ml (7 fl oz) white wine vinegar
50 ml (1¾ fl oz) rice wine vinegar
1 tablespoon sesame oil
2 tablespoons Kikkoman soy sauce
100 g (4 oz) tahini paste
1 tablespoon crushed garlic
sea salt and freshly ground pepper
1½ tablespoons chilli oil
¼ teaspoon chilli paste
sugar to taste

2 spring onions, finely sliced
2 tablespoons toasted sesame seeds

roasted eggplant with feta and anchovy crumbs

As a child I always ate eggplant fried with eggs and bacon. Eggplant and egg yolk are just made to go together, as are all the ingredients in this dish which Ray McVinnie cooked in one of his ongoing 'Around the Tables of the World' series. 'Around the Mediterranean Table' was perhaps one of the most popular classes ever.

preheat the oven to 200°C/400°F.

Paint a baking sheet with the oil, place the eggplant slices on it in a single layer. Sprinkle all over with garlic, salt and pepper. Bake until well browned. Set aside in a warm place.

Arrange all the vegetables, including the eggplant, on a serving platter and drizzle with extra virgin olive oil.

To make the crumbs, heat the olive oil over a medium heat in a large frying pan. Add the crumbs, thyme, garlic and anchovies and stirfry until golden brown.

Sprinkle the fried crumbs over the vegetables. Add the vinegar to the hot pan and let it bubble. Pour this over the vegetables and garnish with extra parsley.

SERVES 4–6

olive oil for brushing

2–3 medium eggplants, sliced 2 cm ($^3/_4$") thick

2 cloves garlic, finely chopped

salt and pepper

1 red onion, sliced

1 cup firm feta, crumbled

500 g (1 lb) small round green beans, trimmed and blanched

1 cup Italian parsley sprigs

extra virgin olive oil

ANCHOVY CRUMBS

4 tablespoons olive oil

2 cups fresh breadcrumbs

1 tablespoon thyme leaves

2 cloves garlic, finely chopped

10 anchovy fillets, chopped

$^1/_2$ cup red wine vinegar

orzo with feta and walnuts

The first time I ever tasted orzo (rice shaped pasta) was when Ray McVinnie prepared this in class. This pasta is equally good served hot, like any pasta, or cold as a salad. This dish was part of a menu designed for Christmas Day – one that looks to the summer and tries to step away from traditional English fare. Each year we ask a different chef to do this class, simply titled 'Festive Fare'.

heat a little olive oil in a skillet over a medium heat and fry the walnuts until golden.

Cook the orzo in abundant boiling, salted water until al dente. Drain and place in a warm serving bowl. Sprinkle over the feta, preserved lemon and walnuts. Top with a good handful of rocket leaves and drizzle with olive oil. Grind over some black pepper and serve immediately.

SERVES 4

1$\frac{1}{4}$ cups fresh walnut halves
extra virgin olive oil
2 cups orzo
170 g (6 oz) firm feta, crumbled
2 quarters of preserved lemon, sliced
  (see page 195)
rocket leaves
sea salt and freshly ground pepper

chilled asparagus, shaved fennel and pecorino
with lemon-basil vinaigrette

Accompanied by nothing more than some good bread, salads can make a meal in their own right. This is one for early summer, when asparagus is at its best. Pecorino is a sheeps milk cheese from Italy. Use Parmesan as an alternative if need be.

blanch the asparagus in boiling water until just tender, remove and immediately plunge into iced water. When chilled, remove and drain well on paper towels. Refrigerate until ready to use – up to 12 hours.

Cut the fennel bulb in half lengthwise. Cut out the tough core and slice crosswise into very thin slices. Drop into cold water to refresh and soften. Refrigerate in water until ready to use – up to 12 hours.

In a food processor blend the lemon juice, zest, garlic, basil, vinegar and sugar. In a thin stream, add the oil and process until well blended. Season to taste with salt and pepper. Use immediately or refrigerate.

When ready to serve, toss the asparagus with about $\frac{1}{3}$ cup of the vinaigrette. Arrange on a platter with all the tips facing the same way.

In the same bowl, toss the drained fennel with a few tablespoons of dressing, then arrange on top of the asparagus.

Sprinkle the chopped tomatoes over the fennel.

With a vegetable peeler, shave curls of pecorino over the salad.

Season with salt and pepper and serve.

SERVES 6

500 g (1 lb) thin asparagus, trimmed
1 large bulb fennel, leaves and stalk removed
handful of cherry tomatoes, halved
60 g (2$\frac{1}{4}$ oz) pecorino cheese, in one piece
sea salt and freshly ground pepper

VINAIGRETTE
$\frac{1}{4}$ cup freshly squeezed lemon juice
1 teaspoon finely chopped lemon zest
2 garlic cloves, roughly chopped
12 leaves fresh basil, roughly chopped
$\frac{1}{4}$ cup red wine vinegar
$\frac{1}{2}$ teaspoon sugar
1 cup extra virgin olive oil
sea salt and freshly ground pepper

quinoa with chervil

The history behind quinoa (pronounced keen-o-a) is one that fascinates me. It's believed to be one of the oldest grains still in use today, having been grown in South America for centuries. It has a delicious nutty flavour and is easily found in health stores.

rinse the quinoa well, then drain. Heat the oil in a pan and gently fry the shallots and garlic for about 3 minutes.

Add the quinoa, currants and almonds and, stirring well, cook for about 2 minutes. Add the hot stock, bring to the boil, then cover and reduce the heat to a gentle simmer. Cook for about 12–15 minutes until all the liquid is absorbed. Remove from the heat and stir in $\frac{1}{2}$ cup of chervil and the lemon zest.

Season well with salt and pepper and leave to stand for 5 minutes. Stir in the remaining chervil and serve.

SERVES 4

1 cup quinoa
2 tablespoons olive oil
3 shallots, finely chopped
2 large garlic cloves, chopped
25 g (1 oz) currants
25 g (1 oz) flaked almonds
300 ml ($\frac{1}{2}$ pint) hot chicken stock
$\frac{1}{2}$ cup plus 2–3 tablespoons chopped chervil
zest of a lemon, chopped
sea salt and freshly ground pepper

raspberry and zinfandel sherbet with warm berry compote

Zinfandel, that famous Californian wine, makes a magnificent sherbet or sorbet. For Joanne Weir this dish is one way to celebrate summer. For us here in New Zealand it would certainly make a beautiful Christmas dessert.

sherbet

bring the Zinfandel, sugar and water to a boil. As soon as it comes to a boil, pour it over the raspberries. Leave to steep for 30 minutes.

Purée the raspberries and Zinfandel mixture in a blender and strain through a fine strainer. Chill the mixture completely.

Churn in an ice-cream machine or pour the mixture into a shallow metal container. Freeze until ice crystals have formed and the mixture is solid around the edge. Blend in a food processor or blender and repeat again at least twice before allowing to freeze completely.

for the compote

purée 1 cup of raspberries in a food processor or blender to obtain a smooth purée. Strain through a fine mesh strainer into a clean bowl.

Place the water, sugar and lemon peel in a medium pan over a high heat and bring to a boil. Reduce the heat to medium and add the blueberries. Cook until the blueberries just begin to crack – about 1 minute. Add the fraises des bois if using. Remove the lemon peel and discard. Stir in the raspberry purée, Cassis and remaining 1 cup of raspberries. Makes 2 cups.

To serve, warm the compote. Scoop the sherbet into bowls and spoon the compote over the top. Serve immediately.

SERVES 6

SHERBET
3 cups fruity white Zinfandel
1 cup plus 2 tablespoons sugar
$\frac{1}{3}$ cup water
6 cups raspberries, washed and hulled

COMPOTE
2 cups raspberries
$\frac{1}{2}$ cup water
$\frac{1}{3}$ cup sugar
1 piece lemon peel, 5 cm (2″) long removed with a vegetable peeler
$\frac{3}{4}$ cup blueberries
$\frac{3}{4}$ cup fraises des bois or wild strawberries (optional)
1 tablespoon Cassis
1 teaspoon lemon juice

walnut cake with blue cheese and pears

At the end of a leisurely lunch, the last thing anyone feels like is a rich dessert. Fruit is always a good option or try this very simple walnut cake and serve it with your favourite blue cheese and the most beautiful pears you can find. It's a 'help yourself' dish to eat with the last of the red wine or with coffee.

preheat the oven to 180°C/350°F. Butter and flour a 20 cm (8") spring-form cake tin and line the base with baking paper.

Beat the butter and sugar together with the orange zest in the bowl of an electric mixer until pale and creamy. Add the eggs, one at a time, beating well after each. Fold through the dry ingredients and the nuts.

Spoon the mixture into the prepared tin and bake for 45 minutes or until a skewer, inserted in the centre, comes out clean.

Cool on a rack.

Serve the cake on a platter with a wedge of blue cheese and ripe pears.

CAKE
180 g (6$\frac{1}{2}$ oz) unsalted butter, melted
180 g (6$\frac{1}{2}$ oz) brown sugar
zest of 1 orange
3 eggs, beaten
180 g (6$\frac{1}{2}$ oz) plain flour, sifted
1 teaspoon baking powder
1$\frac{1}{2}$ cups walnut pieces, chopped

TO SERVE
blue cheese
ripe pears

weekend in the country

The very thought of a weekend in the country conjures up visions of long leisurely meals and delicious hearty food. Long slow cooking, really good bread, puddings and excellent red wines, not to mention good company and conversation, morning lie-ins with a good book and cups of tea in bed. To achieve all of these things, organisation and easy recipes are a must – soups and meat dishes that can be prepared ahead, that actually improve over a couple of days, cakes in the tins that can be served instead of pudding with cheese and fruit.

mushroom soup with little dumplings

Dumplings are rarely seen in modern cookery although they were once a regular alternative to potatoes and a good way of using up stale bread. Here we flavour our dumplings well, with Parmesan and parsley, and roll them into tiny balls which float elegantly in the soup. Make this soup if you've been out collecting field mushrooms on an autumn day.

to make the dumplings, mix all the ingredients together, then form into marble-sized balls by rolling firmly between the palms of your hands. Set aside in a single layer.

cook the bacon in a large saucepan over a medium heat until the fat begins to run. Add the olive oil and butter and when hot add the shallots. Continue cooking until they are soft, but not coloured.

Add the field mushrooms and cook over a low to medium heat, stirring occasionally, and when the juices run and the mushrooms soften, pour in the stock and simmer gently for 25 minutes. Season to taste with salt, pepper and nutmeg.

Drop the dumplings into the soup and cook for 1–2 minutes, then add the mixed mushrooms and cook for 1 minute more. Serve immediately.

SERVES 6–8

DUMPLINGS

3 cups fresh white breadcrumbs

4 egg yolks, beaten

2 tablespoons chopped flatleaf parsley

75 g (2¾ oz) freshly grated Parmesan cheese

freshly ground pepper

SOUP

150 g (5½ oz) streaky bacon

5 tablespoons olive oil

100 g (4 oz) butter

4 shallots, finely chopped

750 g (1¾ lb) field mushrooms, sliced

2 litres (8 cups) chicken stock

sea salt and freshly ground pepper

freshly ground nutmeg

TO SERVE

300 g mixed mushrooms – shiitake, woodear, phoenix, button

caldo verde

This is the sort of soup which warms you right through. It's a very traditional Italian soup which uses those basic ingredients potato and cabbage, enhanced with garlic, spicy sausage and a little olive oil. Eat it with plenty of crusty bread.

place the potatoes and garlic in a large pot with the stock or water and bring to the boil. Reduce the heat and simmer for 15 minutes until the potatoes are tender. Season.

Mash the potatoes in the pot until fairly smooth. Add the slices of sausage and the shredded cabbage. Simmer for about 5 minutes or until warmed through. Taste and adjust seasoning if necessary.

Ladle into large warmed soup bowls. Pour over a tablespoon or so of olive oil in circles on top of each serving. If using coriander, tear a few leaves and scatter over each portion before serving.

SERVES 6

1 kg (2 lb 2oz) potatoes, peeled and diced

2 cloves garlic, chopped

1.5 litres (6 cups) chicken stock or water

225 g (8 oz) chorizo sausage or other semi-dried meaty sausage, sliced 1 cm ($\frac{1}{4}$")

500 g (1 lb) Savoy cabbage or other mild greens, finely shredded

salt and pepper

6 tablespoons extra virgin olive oil

1 tablespoon coriander leaves (optional) to serve

potato gnocchi with creamy blue cheese sauce

Gnocchi are also little dumplings, this time made with potatoes, which take the place of pasta very well. They are incredibly easy to make, and can be served with any favourite pasta sauce.

boil the potatoes until tender.

Just before the potatoes are cooked, sprinkle half the flour directly onto your work surface, covering an area about 25 cm (10") in diameter.

Drain and peel the potatoes while still hot and immediately pass them through a potato ricer, or mouli, onto the flour.

Sprinkle the potato with salt and then with the remaining flour, using a dough scraper and one hand, work the flour into the potato as quickly as possible.

As soon as you have a smooth dough stop working it.

Place the milk and cream into a saucepan or casserole large enough to hold the gnocchi. Bring to the boil, turn the heat to low and add the blue cheese, stirring until it has melted. Turn off the heat until ready to use.

When you begin to cook the gnocchi, heat the sauce gently, stir in the Parmesan cheese and season with salt.

Put a large stockpot of salted water on to boil.

Break off small lumps of the gnocchi dough and roll into a rope measuring about 1.5 cm ($\frac{1}{2}$") in diameter then cut into 2–3 cm (1") lengths. Set aside on a floured surface and repeat with remaining dough.

Drop the gnocchi, in batches, into simmering water. Allow them to rise to the surface, then leave them for 1 minute more before lifting out with a slotted spoon. Drop them immediately into the prepared sauce.

SERVES 6

GNOCCHI

1 kg (2 lb 2 oz) all purpose potatoes such as Desirée, scrubbed
300 g (10$\frac{1}{2}$ oz) plain flour
sea salt

SAUCE

$\frac{1}{2}$ cup (125 ml) milk
$\frac{1}{2}$ cup (125 ml) cream
100 g (4 oz) soft blue cheese
$\frac{1}{3}$ cup freshly grated Parmesan cheese
sea salt

ENTERTAINING
EPICUREAN

tuscan country pasta with ricotta

The ricotta makes this a creamy, but not rich sauce. Although this cannot be made ahead and reheated, it is possible to have the ingredients prepared to the point where all that is needed is to add the cooking water. Serve with plenty of bread and a crisp salad.

heat the olive oil in a medium-sized heavy skillet. Add the onion and bacon and cook over a low heat until the onion is soft and translucent and the bacon renders its fat but is not yet crisp. Remove from the heat and set aside.

In a small mixing bowl beat the ricotta, parsley, basil, spring onion tops and Parmesan cheese. Add the onion, bacon and its fat, and salt and pepper to taste. Mix well.

Bring a large pot of water to a rolling boil, add salt and cook the rigatoni until al dente. While the pasta is cooking, add $\frac{1}{4}$ to $\frac{1}{2}$ cup of the cooking water to the ricotta mixture. Mix well.

Drain the pasta in a colander and place it in a shallow serving bowl. Add the ricotta mixture and toss.

Serve immediately, passing additional Parmesan cheese.

SERVES 4–6

$\frac{1}{4}$ **cup extra virgin olive oil**
1 onion, chopped
2 rashers bacon, coarsely chopped
450 g (16 oz) ricotta
$\frac{1}{4}$ **cup Italian parsley, coarsely chopped**
handful of basil leaves, coarsely chopped
1 tablespoon spring onion tops, finely chopped
$\frac{1}{4}$ **cup Parmesan cheese, grated**
salt and pepper to taste
450 g (16 oz) dried rigatoni pasta

paella with chicken, seafood and chorizo sausage

My first paella experience was fun. Four of us sat all alone in an enormous dining room in a hotel on the northern coast of Spain. It was too early in the summer for this beach-side town to be busy. We ordered our paella and between us polished off a dish which could have fed 12, it was so good. The waitress became remarkably upset when we explained we did not want any other courses. The paella, apparently, was meant to be just the first! Later on that same trip, at a campsite one night, I watched an elderly man make a fire and proceed to cook a rabbit paella. He made it look so easy and it is.

Paella is a dish that can be cooked and enjoyed no matter what the season. In summer, prepare it outside on the barbecue and in winter let everyone share in its cooking around the stove. Then, take the whole pan to the table.

heat the chicken stock, add the saffron threads and allow to infuse.

Heat the oil in a large heavy-based ovenproof pan or paella dish over a high heat.

Add the chicken and sauté to brown.

Add the sausage and sauté until coloured. Toss in the onion, capsicum and courgettes and cook for a further 2 minutes.

Add the seafood and garlic, cooking until the mussels open and the prawns are pink, then remove the seafood and set aside.

Add the rice and stir well to coat the grains with oil. Pour in the chicken stock, tomatoes and zest, bring to the boil and reduce the heat to a gentle simmer.

Cook uncovered for 20 minutes. Five minutes before the end put the seafood on top of the rice. Cover with tinfoil and stand in a warm place for another 10 minutes.

To serve, remove the foil and garnish with lemon wedges and parsley.

SERVES 6

1¼ litres (5 cups) chicken stock
pinch of saffron threads, toasted
6 tablespoons olive oil
250 g (9 oz) boneless chicken thighs, cut into 2.5 cm (1") pieces
200 g (7 oz) chorizo sausage, sliced ½ cm (¼")
1 red onion, cut into 2.5 cm (1") pieces
1 red capsicum, cut into 2.5 cm (1") chunks
2 courgettes, sliced
6 large green prawns
12 mussels, cleaned and debearded
5 cloves garlic, chopped
2½ cups shortgrain rice, preferably Calasparra or Arborio
1 x 400 g (14 oz) tin whole peeled Italian tomatoes, drained and roughly chopped
zest of 2 lemons
chopped Italian parsley and lemon wedges for garnish

garlic roast chicken with fennel and onions

A whole roast chicken is still one of life's pleasures, even though it is one of the simplest ways to prepare poultry. The method in this recipe is a little different – browning the chicken first is certainly not traditional, but the results are amazing – melting vegetables and succulent chicken.

preheat the oven to 220°C/425°F.

Trim the fennel and cut into wedges.

Rub the chicken all over with 2 cloves of crushed garlic and the thyme. Season with salt and pepper. Place the rosemary and 3 whole peeled cloves of garlic in the cavity.

Melt the butter together with the oil in a roasting pan over a medium heat.

Add the chicken and brown well on all sides. Add the fennel and onions to the pan and season lightly. Add $\frac{1}{4}$ cup of the stock and roast in the oven for 45 minutes, adding a little more stock as necessary and basting every 10 minutes. Turn the fennel several times.

When the chicken is cooked, transfer to a platter with the vegetables. Add the remaining stock to the pan and bring to the boil on top of the stove. Reduce a little, season and spoon over the vegetables. Garnish with chopped fennel tops or parsley.

Serve with a salad and some bread to mop up the sauce.

SERVES 6

500 g (1 lb) fennel bulb (about 2 medium bulbs)
1.5 kg (3$\frac{1}{2}$ lb) cornfed chicken
5 large cloves garlic
1 tablespoon fresh thyme
salt and freshly ground pepper
sprig fresh rosemary
2 tablespoons butter
1 tablespoon extra virgin olive oil
4–6 small onions, unpeeled and cut in half crosswise
375 ml (1$\frac{1}{2}$ cups) chicken stock
fennel tops or Italian parsley

lamb shank 'mirmiz' with creamy polenta

Kate Fay cooked these lamb shanks in a class about cosy winter food called 'Comfort Zones'. Buy shanks that have had the bone cleaned – this dispenses with some very tough sinew and looks far more attractive on the plate. The Middle Eastern tones of this dish suggest pita bread as an appropriate accompaniment, but I would also serve it with creamy polenta, as Kate did, or even couscous.

preheat the oven to 190°C/375°F.

In a large frying pan, sear the lamb shanks in the olive oil. Place in a roasting dish.

In a separate pot sauté the onion and leek and add the other ingredients. Pour this mixture over the lamb shanks. Cover with tinfoil and cook for approximately 2 hours until the lamb is tender.

Serve with the creamy polenta on page 195, couscous or pita bread.

SERVES 8

8 lamb shanks

2 tablespoons olive oil

2 onions, finely sliced

1 leek, finely sliced

3 tablespoons coriander seeds, toasted and ground

1 tablespoon cumin seeds, toasted and ground

2 dried chillies, ground

2 teaspoons cracked pepper

$\frac{1}{2}$ teaspoon harissa (optional)

2 tablespoons paprika

100 g (4 oz) soaked chickpeas

2 x 400 g (14 oz) tins tomatoes and their juices

1.5 litres ($2\frac{3}{4}$ pints) beef stock

2 teaspoons crushed garlic

tuscan chicken

The idea for this dish came from The New Basics, a revolutionary book published at least 10 years ago now. It soon became a favourite which I also taught, way back in 1993, in a class called 'What to Have for Dinner'. Sometimes, instead of polenta, I just serve a basket of bread and always a green salad afterwards, on clean plates.

cut the chicken into 8 pieces.

In a large ceramic dish, combine the red wine, celery, shallots, olives, sultanas and capers. Add the chicken pieces and dried herbs and season. Cover and refrigerate overnight or for at least 2 hours.

Preheat the oven to 180°C/350°F.

Heat the oil in a heavy-based, oven-proof frying pan or casserole. Remove the chicken from the marinade and brown well in the hot oil. Reserve the marinade.

Mix the tomato paste and stock together and add to the marinade. When all the chicken is browned, pour this mixture over, increase the heat and bring to the boil.

Transfer the frying pan to the oven and bake for 30–40 minutes, basting once or twice, until the chicken is cooked and the juices run clear.

Bring the frying pan to the table and serve at once with grilled polenta.

SERVES 4

1.5–2 kg ($3\frac{1}{2}$ – $4\frac{1}{2}$ lb) cornfed chicken or 8 chicken pieces
$\frac{3}{4}$ cup red wine
3 stalks celery, sliced
6 shallots, quartered
15 black olives, pitted
$\frac{1}{3}$ cup sultanas
$\frac{1}{4}$ cup capers
1 teaspoon dried sage
1 teaspoon dried rosemary
sea salt and freshly ground pepper
1 tablespoon extra virgin olive oil
$\frac{1}{4}$ cup tomato paste
$\frac{3}{4}$ cup chicken or beef stock

country style vegetable stew

A vegetable stew like this one makes a perfect alternative to a savoury tart or pie and is far easier to produce. Other seasonal vegetables such as courgettes, beans or asparagus can be included, but may need to be added towards the end of cooking to preserve their texture and colour. Any white beans are suitable, although my preference is for baby lima.

place the olive oil, garlic, onion, celery, rosemary and saffron in a large sauté pan and cook over a medium heat until the vegetables are soft – about 5 minutes.

Add the remaining vegetables and the chilli. Season and cover tightly. Cook over a low heat for 30 minutes, stirring occasionally, adding a little water if the mixture appears dry.

Add the beans during the last 5 minutes of cooking.

Stir in the remaining herbs and remove from the heat.

Serve warm or at room temperature in big bowls with plenty of good bread.

SERVES 6

5 tablespoons extra virgin olive oil
2 cloves garlic, crushed
1 onion, sliced thickly
2 stalks celery, sliced
1 teaspoon finely chopped rosemary
small pinch saffron threads
1 small eggplant, diced 2 cm ($^3/_4$")
2 yellow capsicums, seeded and sliced
2 medium, waxy potatoes, diced 2 cm ($^3/_4$")
1x 400 g (14 oz) tin tomatoes
1 small red chilli, seeded and finely chopped
sea salt and freshly ground pepper
1$^1/_2$ cups cooked white beans
2 tablespoons chopped Italian parsley
2 tablespoons chopped basil

springfield pear cake with whisky sauce

Ruth Pretty is a well known name in New Zealand catering circles. She produces food for the rich and famous from her custom built kitchens adjacent to her home of 'Springfield', at Te Horo, just north of Wellington. The pears which inspired this cake are grown in an orchard on the property. Ruth shared this recipe with us in a class about country weekend cooking, so it's very appropriate that we include it here. It makes a large cake, but it's one that keeps well.

preheat the oven to 180°C/350°F. Butter and flour a 10-cup capacity kugelhopf cake tin.

Place the sultanas and water in a saucepan and bring to the boil over a low heat. Simmer for 3–4 minutes. Remove from the heat and stir in the pears, whisky and baking soda. Cool.

In an electric mixer fitted with a K beater (paddle), cream together the butter and sugar until light and fluffy. Gradually add the beaten eggs and vanilla, beating continuously.

Sift together the flour, baking powder, cloves and mixed spice. Spoon half the dry ingredients and half the pear mixture over the creamed mixture. Stir gently to combine. Repeat with the remaining dry ingredients and the pear mixture.

Spoon the mixture into the prepared tin and bake for 50–60 minutes or until a skewer inserted comes out clean. Leave the cake in the tin for 10 minutes before turning out onto a platter.

To make the whisky sauce, put the milk, cream and vanilla bean into a heavy-based saucepan and bring to boiling point.

Whisk the egg yolks and caster sugar until pale and thick.

Pour the scalded milk and cream over the egg mixture, whisking continuously.

Return the custard to the pot and cook (over a gentle heat) until the mixture coats the back of the spoon (do not allow the mixture to boil as it will curdle). Strain the custard through a fine sieve. Add the whisky and stir to combine. Chill until required.

Serve the cake hot, warm or cold, dusted with icing sugar and accompanied by whisky sauce and whipped cream.

SERVES 10-12

230 g (1½ cups) sultanas

250 ml (1 cup) water

485 g (3 cups) roughly chopped, peeled pears

125 ml (½ cup) whisky

½ teaspoon baking soda

190 g (6½ oz) butter

240 g (1 cup) caster sugar

2 eggs, lightly beaten

1½ teaspoons pure vanilla extract

350 g (12 oz) plain flour

1 tablespoon baking powder

¾ teaspoon ground cloves

1½ teaspoons mixed spice

WHISKY SAUCE

150 ml (¼ pint) milk

150 ml (¼ pint) cream

½ vanilla bean, split in half lengthways

4 egg yolks

80 g (2¾ oz) caster sugar

60 ml (¼ cup) whisky

MAKES 600 ML

panna cotta with pears baked in verjuice

Panna cotta is another 'new' dessert which has become as popular as crème brulée on restaurant menus. The secret with panna cotta is to use minimal gelatine. This 'cooked cream' should be softly set, firm enough to fall out of the mould intact but not stiff like a firm jelly. The pears for poaching should be very hard, unripe pears. Long, slow cooking results in a translucent, soft and absolutely delicious fruit. I attribute this recipe to Maggie Beer and Stephanie Alexander. It is one of the many wonderful dishes I cooked with them in Italy.

place the cream, vanilla pod and sugar in a pot and heat gently over a low heat until the sugar is dissolved. Remove the vanilla pod. Dissolve the softened gelatine over warm water and add, mixing well. Stir occasionally until cool. Pour into 6 individual moulds and chill for 4–6 hours or overnight until firm.

Place the verjuice and sugar in a heavy-based saucepan and dissolve the sugar over a low heat.

Increase the heat and bring to the boil. Boil steadily until the liquid is syrupy.

Preheat the oven to 150°C/300°F.

Peel, quarter and core the pears, placing them in acidulated water (water and lemon juice) as you go, to prevent discolouration.

Remove them from the water and place in an ovenproof baking dish. Pour over the verjuice syrup, making sure the syrup covers the pears, and bake, turning and basting occasionally, until the pears are tender and translucent. This will take anything from an hour to 2 hours, depending on the pears. Cool in the syrup.

Turn out the panna cotta onto serving plates and serve with the pears and a little of the poaching syrup.

SERVES 6

PANNA COTTA
1 litre (1¾ pints) cream
1 vanilla pod, split
8 teaspoons castor sugar
3 teaspoons powdered gelatine, softened in a little water

PEARS
375 ml (1½ cups) verjuice or dry white wine
375 g (13 oz) sugar
6 whole hard pears

a long lunch

Europeans know all about 'the long lunch'. For them it is an important tradition – one that involves families and friends gathering around a table to enjoy food and wine together, something that many people have forgotten how to do. A long lunch has few requirements – a long table (which can be indoors or out), lots of good food in the middle, plenty of wine, laughter and stories. Remember, you can have a long lunch anywhere, not just in Italy or France.

sicilian marinated olives

Olives marinated this way are a delicious nibble with a glass of wine before a meal. They also make a good addition to an antipasti platter or salad. Kalamata olives are recognised by their pointed ends.

if the surface of each olive has not already been pierced, do so with the point of a small knife. This allows the flavours in the oil to permeate.

Combine all the ingredients together in a clean, dry jar and leave to marinate at room temperature for 24 hours. Store in the fridge.

To serve, remove the olives from the oil and drain.

500 g (1 lb) Kalamata olives
8 garlic cloves, cut lengthways
julienned zest of $\frac{1}{2}$ orange
julienned zest of $\frac{1}{2}$ lemon
2 tablespoons fennel seeds
2 tablespoons fresh rosemary
juice of 2 lemons
150 ml (5$\frac{1}{2}$ fl oz) olive oil

green olive 'fritters'

Find the very best green olives for these 'fritters'. They will be unstoned but the flavour will be infinitely better.

drain the olives and dry on paper towels. Mix the breadcrumbs and Parmesan together.

Heat 2.5 cm (1") of olive oil in a heavy pan over a medium heat.

Dredge the olives in flour, then dip into the beaten egg and roll in the breadcrumb mix.

Immediately fry the olives in batches for 1 minute or until pale gold. Remove with a slotted spoon and drain on paper towels. Keep olives warm while frying the remainder in batches. Serve warm with a glass of wine.

250 g (9 oz) good quality, large green olives
100 g (4 oz) fresh breadcrumbs
100 g (4 oz) fresh, finely grated Parmesan cheese
olive oil for frying
200 g (7 oz) plain flour
2 eggs, lightly beaten

gorgonzola risotto balls

Gabriele Ferron introduced us to these little morsels during his visit in 1999. Using the no-stir Ferron method (page 194) cuts down the preparation time and, what's more, they can be made ahead and gently reheated.

heat a little olive oil in a heavy-based pan and sauté the onion until soft and translucent, but not coloured. Add the rice and toss to coat with oil. Stir gently until the rice is hot (toasted).

Add the hot stock and milk, cover the pan and reduce the heat to a simmer. Cook the rice for 15 minutes, stirring once. After 12 minutes add the gorgonzola.

Remove from the heat and add the egg yolk. Season well and mix to combine. Spread out onto a tray and allow to cool. Cover with plastic wrap and refrigerate until well chilled.

Roll into small balls, the size of a cherry. When ready to cook, toss them first in flour, then beaten egg and lastly in the breadcrumbs.

Heat enough olive oil to cover the base of the pan to a depth of $\frac{1}{2}$ cm ($\frac{1}{4}$"). Fry the risotto balls until golden and serve hot.

MAKES 35–40

1 tablespoon extra virgin olive oil
1 onion, chopped
1 cup Vialano Nano rice
200 ml (7 fl oz) chicken stock, hot
200 ml (7 fl oz) milk, hot
130 g (41/2 oz) gorgonzola cheese
1 egg yolk
sea salt and freshly ground pepper
flour
2 eggs, beaten
very fine toasted breadcrumbs
olive oil for frying

sicilian swordfish rolls

These ingredients are particularly indicative of Sicily – the pinenuts, currants and citrus are just some of the influences that are unique to this small island's cuisine. It's a very pretty dish. I love the way the bayleaves poke out from between each roll. Serve it at room temperature for the best flavour.

sauté the onion in the olive oil until soft and golden – about 10 minutes. Add the breadcrumbs and cook until golden. Remove from the heat and add the currants, pinenuts and parsley. Add the juices, taste and add sugar if necessary. Season and leave to cool.

Heat the oven to 190°C/375°F. Brush a 20 x 30 cm (8 x 12″) shallow baking dish with olive oil.

Spread the fish slices out (if too thick, flatten with a rolling pin between 2 sheets of waxed paper). Sprinkle the fish with salt. Place a tablespoon of the filling on each slice and roll up. Place rolls side by side in the prepared dish and sprinkle with the remaining filling and the olive oil. Stick bayleaves between each roll and at the end of each row.

Bake in the centre of the oven for 15 minutes or until the fish is opaque and just cooked through. Serve warm or at room temperature.

SERVES 6

FILLING

1 medium red onion, finely chopped

100 ml (3$\frac{1}{2}$ fl oz) olive oil

5 tablespoons fresh white breadcrumbs

5 tablespoons currants, soaked in warm water for 5 minutes

5 tablespoons pinenuts

$\frac{1}{2}$ bunch Italian parsley, finely chopped

2 tablespoons each orange and lemon juice

pinch sugar, optional

salt and freshly ground black pepper

12 thin slices swordfish, about 6 mm ($\frac{1}{4}$″) thick, or light flesh of tuna or fresh sardines, gutted

4 tablespoons extra virgin olive oil

16 fresh bayleaves

63

sugar cured beef, pesto beans and black olive oil

Geoff Lindsay has twice been a guest at Epicurean and on each occasion has wowed us with his food. Both the beef and the beans in this dish are good to serve in their own right, but together they make music. Szechwan peppercorns are available at Asian supermarkets. In the interests of time I would purchase the pesto and onions from a good deli.

roll the beef in thyme and peppercorns, ensuring an even cover.

Combine the sugar, salt and brandy and pack around the beef so it is completely enclosed.

Refrigerate and turn every 12 hours for 48 hours.

Remove from the brine and pat dry.

Purée the olives in a blender with the oil.

Strain through a fine sieve, pushing the olive paste through to form a thick oil.

Blanch the beans in rapidly boiling water until tender. Mix with the pesto and while still warm add the sundried tomato and pickled onions.

Place a pile of the pesto beans on a serving plate.

Slice the beef finely and drape a few slices over the beans.

Drizzle the plate and the meat with black olive oil.

Serve while the pesto beans are still warm.

SERVES 6–8

500 g (1 lb) eye fillet of beef, trimmed of all fat and silverskin
1 tablespoon chopped fresh thyme
100 g (4 oz) crushed peppercorns (mixture of black, white, Szechwan)
150 g (5$\frac{1}{2}$ oz) sugar
250 g (9 oz) rock salt
50 ml (1$\frac{3}{4}$ fl oz) brandy

BLACK OLIVE OIL
50 g (1$\frac{3}{4}$ oz) Ligurian olives, pitted
100 ml (3$\frac{1}{2}$ fl oz) extra virgin olive oil

PESTO BEANS
250 g (9 oz) tiny French beans
2 heaped tablespoons pesto
50 g (1$\frac{3}{4}$ oz) sundried tomatoes, cut in strips
50 g (1$\frac{3}{4}$ oz) small wild pickled onions, cut in quarters

arista

Last time I was in Italy I assisted in the cooking of a huge loin of pork, using a paste similar to this one. In my version the pork fillets require little preparation and have a much shorter cooking time – perfect for busy people. Resting is an important step which will result in moist, succulent meat.

preheat the oven to 200°C/400°F.

Using a mortar and pestle or small food processor, make a paste with the garlic, fennel seeds, salt and pepper.

Spread the paste all over the pork fillets and drizzle with a little olive oil.

Roast the pork uncovered for approximately 15 minutes or until the juices run clear. Baste once or twice with the pan juices during cooking.

Remove from the oven and rest, lightly covered, for 10 minutes. Slice and serve with a further drizzle of olive oil, some crunchy sage potatoes and a salad.

SERVES 6–8

6 cloves garlic, crushed

1–2 tablespoons fennel seeds

2 teaspoons coarse salt

freshly ground pepper

4 pork fillets, about 300 g (10 oz)
   each, trimmed of any sinew

extra virgin olive oil

broad beans with peas and fennel

We converted a surprising number of people to broad beans with this dish. The secret is to remove the thick skin around each bean. Most people's dislike of this vegetable stems from childhood and the pile of grey leathery beans that would be left till last and pushed to the side of the plate with a defiant 'No'. They were certainly one of the very few foods I refused to eat as a child. Serve this dish hot or at room temperature.

heat the oil and butter in a heavy-based casserole or sauté pan. Add the onion and sauté gently for a few minutes. Add the fennel and sauté for a few minutes more. Add the broad beans and peas, cover and cook just until heated through, stirring from time to time.
Season with salt and pepper.

SERVES 6

2 tablespoons extra virgin olive oil
2 tablespoons unsalted butter
1 large onion, thinly sliced
1 large fennel bulb, thinly sliced
500 g (1 lb) frozen broad beans, blanched, well drained and peeled
2 cups frozen peas, blanched and well drained
sea salt and freshly ground pepper

fennel and rocket in white wine

Whereas fennel was a minor ingredient in our broad bean dish, in this one Julie le Clerc made it the hero. Fennel is an interesting vegetable, with its subtle anise flavour and its celery like composition. It can also be sliced thinly and eaten raw in salads, roasted Italian style in olive oil, or braised in chicken stock.

trim the fennel bulbs. Slice in half and then cut into thin segments.
Put all the ingredients, except the rocket, into a sauté pan. Cover and bring to the boil then cook uncovered at a steady simmer until the fennel is tender and the liquid has almost totally evaporated. Lastly toss through the shredded rocket to wilt. Remove the cinnamon stick and bayleaves and serve immediately as a hot vegetable.
This can also be served cold as a salad or antipasto dish.

SERVES 8

1.5 kg (3½ lb) fennel bulbs
400 ml (14 fl oz) dry white wine
1 tablespoon extra virgin olive oil
2 tablespoons sugar
1 teaspoon salt
1 cinnamon stick
3 bayleaves
juice of 2 lemons
1 bunch rocket, shredded

tuscan grape bread

A few years ago, I stayed with South Australian chef Maggie Beer at her home in the Barossa Valley. Maggie had recently been our guest at the Epicurean. Arriving home inspired after our few days in culinary heaven, I cooked a special menu for 'Gourmet on the Run' in memory of my visit. Included was this sweet bread, taken from Maggie's book, Maggie's Farm.

to make the sponge – stir the yeast and sugar into the warm milk and allow to stand for 10 minutes until frothy. Whisk in the eggs, then stir in the flour a little at a time. Cover tightly with plastic wrap and let stand until bubbly – about 30-45 minutes.

For the dough, stir the flour, sugar and salt into the sponge. Add the butter, a little at a time, and then knead on a lightly floured bench for 6–7 minutes. The dough will be soft, quite sticky and shiny.

Preheat the oven to 220°C/425°F. Lightly oil a 33 x 23 cm (13 x 9") baking pan with walnut oil.

Turn the dough out into the prepared pan, stretching it towards the edges as if making a focaccia.

Toss the grapes and walnuts generously over the dough. Cover with a towel and let rise until double in size.

Bake for 15 minutes, reduce the oven to 200°C/400°F and sprinkle the brown sugar on the top. Bake another 15–20 minutes, watching carefully so the sugar does not burn. Cool on a rack.

SERVES 6

SPONGE
1 tablespoon fresh yeast or 1$\frac{1}{2}$ teaspoons active dried yeast
2 tablespoons sugar
1 cup warm milk
2 eggs
250 g (9 oz) plain flour

DOUGH
250 g (9 oz) plain flour
2 tablespoons sugar
1 teaspoon sea salt
100 g (4 oz) unsalted butter, at room temperature

TOPPING
5 cups red grapes
2 cups walnuts, toasted and skins rubbed off
1$\frac{1}{2}$ tablespoons dark brown sugar

zabaglione with marsala raisins

The English have custard, the French sabayon and the Italians zabaglione. It's a fascinating thing to make – as you whisk you can watch the volume increase until you have a light, airy, but still remarkably creamy 'mousse'. The addition of whipped cream in this version stabilises the mixture and allows it to be held, chilled, until ready to eat.

place the raisins in a small saucepan with the lemon peel, cinnamon stick and Marsala. Heat gently then leave to macerate for 1 hour.

Beat the egg yolks and sugar together in a large heat-proof bowl. Add the white wine and stir to combine. Place the bowl over a pot of simmering water and whisk continuously until the mixture becomes thick and creamy.

Stir through the raisins, cool and then fold in the whipped cream. Spoon the zabaglione into small cups or glasses and chill.

SERVES 6–8

2 tablespoons large plump raisins

small strip lemon peel

5 cm (2″) long cinnamon stick

$\frac{1}{2}$ cup Marsala

3 egg yolks

3 tablespoons sugar

$\frac{1}{2}$ cup dry white wine

$\frac{1}{2}$ cup whipped cream

polenta, almond and lemon cake

Serve this cake with a Late Harvest Riesling or strong coffee at the end of a long lunch. The strained yoghurt is a far more interesting accompaniment than plain whipped cream, but if you have good Greek style yoghurt available locally use it instead of making your own. Occasionally I add a swirl of home-made lemon curd too. Polenta flour is sometimes called fine cornmeal or more confusingly cornflour. The yellow colour will help to differentiate it from the cornflour we use as a thickening agent.

preheat the oven to 160°C/320°F. Butter and flour a 30 cm (12") cake tin and line the base with baking paper.

Beat the butter and sugar together until pale and creamy. Stir through the ground almonds and vanilla. Beat in the eggs, one at a time. Fold in the zest and juice, the polenta, baking powder and salt.

Spoon into the prepared tin and bake for 45–50 minutes or until a skewer inserted in the centre comes out clean. The top will be deep golden.

Cool on a rack.

Line a sieve with clean, wet muslin. Place it over a bowl and pour in the yoghurt. Cover and refrigerate overnight. Next day, discard the whey that has drained into the bowl. Transfer the yoghurt to a bowl and fold through half as much lightly whipped cream.

Serve the cake warm or cold with the yoghurt.

SERVES 10–12

450 g (16 oz) unsalted butter, softened
450 g (16 oz) caster sugar
450 g (16 oz) ground almonds
2 teaspoons vanilla extract
6 eggs
zest of 4 lemons, finely grated
juice of 1 lemon
225 g (8 oz) polenta flour
1½ teaspoons baking powder
¼ teaspoon salt

1 litre plain, unsweetened yoghurt
cream

barbecue

Barbecue classes have become obligatory every term at the Epicurean cookschool, even in winter. It is the only class that attracts more men than women and although I am careful to warn 'no charred chops or sausages here', most are completely surprised at the variety and versatility of the dishes we prepare. Ray McVinnie has been the resident barbecue expert at Epicurean for several years. He more often cooks over wood than gas and has a deep understanding of the process of barbecuing. Barbecue is a tradition New Zealanders have firmly embraced but until now without any great degree of sophistication when it comes to the food. What do I love about it? I can prepare everything ahead – make the salads, marinate or skewer the meat – and relax while someone else does the cooking. Joy!

grilled yoghurt bread with aromatic seeds

There is nothing more delicious than bread fresh from the grill. Hot and with that wonderful grilled flavour, it is perfect to serve with antipasti platters or with a salad. This particular bread calls for goats milk yoghurt, readily available these days. Regular, plain, unsweetened yoghurt is an acceptable alternative.

sprinkle the yeast over the warm water and leave for 10 minutes. Stir in the yoghurt and the high-grade flour. Cover the bowl and sit it in a warm place for 20 minutes. Add the plain flour, salt and 2 tablespoons of oil and mix together. Knead for 1–2 minutes. The dough should be moist but not too sticky. Place 1 tablespoon of oil in a bowl and add the dough, turning to coat. Cover and leave in a warm place for 30 minutes.

Preheat the barbecue or grill to medium high.

Gently knock back the dough and divide into 12 equal portions. Gently roll each portion out, sprinkle with aromatic seeds and a little salt and roll once more to press them in.

Grill until golden – about 2–3 minutes each side.

Serve immediately.

MAKES 12

$\frac{1}{2}$ cup (125 ml) warm water

2 teaspoons dry yeast

1 cup (250 ml) goats milk yoghurt

1$\frac{1}{2}$ cups high-grade (bread) flour

2$\frac{1}{2}$ cups plain (cake) flour

1 teaspoon sea salt

2 tablespoons vegetable oil plus 1 tablespoon

$\frac{1}{4}$ cup cumin or fennel seeds

chicken livers with sweet soy and spring onion

Chicken livers were breakfast food when I was a child and it was not until I was older that I discovered how versatile they really were. I follow the same two rules when cooking any offal. The livers must not have been frozen. Freezing changes the texture totally, making them rather unpleasant in the mouth. And I only just cook them through so they'll stay tender and succulent.

thread the chicken livers and spring onions alternately (4–5 livers per skewer) and place in a shallow glass or ceramic dish.

Mix the soy, mirin, sugar and ginger juice together and pour over the skewers. Cover and marinate, refrigerated, for 30 minutes or up to 2 hours.

Preheat the hotplate on a barbecue and spray or brush with oil. Grill the skewers over a moderate heat for 5–8 minutes, brushing from time to time with the marinade.

Pile onto a platter and serve immediately.

MAKES 12 SKEWERS

500 g (1 lb) fresh chicken livers, trimmed of any fat and sinew
4–5 spring onions, sliced in 2cm (1") lengths
2$\frac{1}{2}$ tablespoons Japanese soy sauce
5 tablespoons mirin or dry sherry
2 tablespoons sugar
3 tablespoons ginger juice, squeezed from grated ginger
bamboo skewers soaked in water

italian bread skewers with pancetta and feta

This is an easy little pre-dinner snack to make on the barbecue. The skewers can be assembled and brushed with the herb oil several hours ahead.

chop the herbs finely and mix with a little olive oil. Season well with salt and pepper.

Brush all the skewer ingredients well with the herbed oil and thread onto the skewers.

When ready to serve, grill on the barbecue or under the grill, turning until all sides are well coloured and the bread and pancetta are crisp.

Serve immediately, piled on a platter.

MAKES 12

12 short bamboo skewers (soaked in water)
12 slices Italian bacon (pancetta) or streaky English bacon
24 small wedges of good bread
12 small pieces feta cheese
24 fresh sage leaves
12 small cherry tomatoes (optional)

fresh herbs – basil, rosemary, parsley
olive oil
salt and freshly ground pepper

75

seafood grill

Ray McVinnie could almost be called our resident barbecue expert. Each term he comes up with another menu of inspired dishes to cook, either partially or entirely on the grill. These 'surprise' parcels can be prepared ahead and refrigerated ready to be grilled.

carefully mix the seafood with the herbs, salt, pepper and olive oil. Set aside to marinate for 30 minutes.

Oil 6 x 30 cm (12 ") squares of tinfoil with a little olive oil. Divide the marinated seafood and the vegetables evenly between the tinfoil squares. Sprinkle each with about 2 tablespoons of white wine.

Close each package and seal tightly. Barbecue on a hot grill for 10 minutes.

Serve with a slice of grilled French bread that has been brushed with olive oil, salt, pepper and chopped garlic.

SERVES 6

SEAFOOD

6 x 100 g (4 oz) pieces skinned, boned firm white fish (snapper, hapuku, john dory or tarakihi)
12 oysters, shelled
12 large prawns, peeled and butterflied
3 cloves garlic, finely chopped
2 tablespoons fresh thyme leaves
sea salt and freshly ground black pepper
100 ml (3$\frac{1}{2}$ fl oz) extra virgin olive oil, plus extra

VEGETABLES

18 spinach leaves, quickly wilted in boiling water, refreshed in cold water and drained
2 cups mushrooms, sliced thinly
6 tomatoes, peeled, cored, seeded and roughly chopped
3 spring onions, finely sliced
white wine

grilled tuna with herbed tomato, garlic oil and lemon sauce

This is the sort of dish I cook on weeknights in the summer. A simple uncooked sauce cum salad and just one thing that needs cooking. Tuna is the ideal fish for the barbecue. Firm fleshed, it stays intact on a hot grill, browning up nicely on the outside and remaining rare inside. Remember, tuna that is cooked through completely will be dry and unpalatable. Serve a slice of good bread on the side or turn the whole dish into a pasta sauce. Just toss the sauce and the tuna, sliced, through hot cooked pasta.

to prepare the sauce, combine the tomatoes, olive oil, lemon juice and garlic in a bowl. Stir to blend. Season with salt and pepper to taste and set aside to let the flavours blend. Just before cooking the tuna, add the herbs and stir to blend.

Preheat the grill. Brush the tuna with olive oil. Cook the tuna for just 1 minute on each side. The tuna will be very rosy and rare on the inside and charred on the outside.

Remove the tuna to a large preheated platter and top with the sauce. Or, slice the tuna into thick strips and serve topped with sauce.

SERVES 4

4 thick tuna steaks
1 tablespoon extra virgin olive oil

SAUCE
3 tomatoes, peeled, cored, seeded and chopped
$\frac{1}{2}$ cup (125 ml) extra virgin olive oil
3 tablespoons lemon juice
3 cloves garlic, finely chopped
sea salt and freshly ground pepper
large handfuls of fresh herbs (mix of chervil, chives, tarragon and parsley)

turkish style grilled chicken with yoghurt and cumin

Turkey is best known for its fragrant dishes that are aromatic, rather than spicy. This simple chicken dish uses yoghurt as a tenderiser and a medium for the spices. Serve with pita bread or rice pilaf and a quick yoghurt sauce made from plain yoghurt, lemon juice, garlic and fresh, chopped mint leaves.

place the chicken thighs in a shallow dish.

Place the cumin, onion, garlic, paprika and lemon juice in the food processor or blender and blend to a pulp. Add the yoghurt and pulse briefly to combine.

Pour over the chicken and toss well to coat. Cover and marinate for 1 hour or overnight in the refrigerator.

Preheat the barbecue.

Season the chicken with salt and pepper and barbecue until it is golden and the juices run clear – about 6 minutes each side.

Garnish with lemon wedges, black olives and Italian parsley leaves.

SERVES 6

12 boneless chicken thighs, skin on
2 tablespoons cumin seeds, toasted
 and ground
1 small onion, chopped
4–6 cloves garlic, crushed
1 tablespoon paprika
juice of 1 lemon
1 cup plain, unsweetened yoghurt
sea salt and freshly ground pepper
lemon wedges, a few black olives and
 Italian parsley leaves to garnish

grilled star anise chicken on wilted greens

We do a lot of grilling in our 'Gourmet on the Run' classes. After all, the purpose of these classes is fast and fairly easy food, so what better cooking method to use? Chicken thighs are my preferred cut for barbecuing. They have good flavour and a little fat to keep the meat succulent while cooking. I always grill them with the skin on because it protects the meat as it grills, but, can, if preferred, be removed before eating.

arrange the chicken thighs, skin-side down, in a shallow dish. Combine the ketjap manis, soy sauce, rice wine, palm sugar, pepper, star anise and cinnamon sticks and heat gently until the palm sugar has melted. Allow to cool, then pour over the chicken, cover and marinate in the refrigerator for up to 24 hours.

When ready to cook, heat the barbecue to a medium-high heat and oil well with peanut oil. Grill the chicken, turning once, for about 10 minutes until well browned and the juices run clear when the chicken is pierced with a small knife. Remove from the grill and rest, covered loosely, for 10 minutes.

While the chicken is grilling, transfer the marinade to a saucepan and reduce until syrupy. Set aside.

Combine the sesame oil, soy sauce, water and sesame seeds and mix well. Brush the mixture onto the prepared greens and grill just until heated through.

Arrange the greens on a platter.

Brush the chicken with the reduced marinade, then slice diagonally and arrange on top of the greens. Serve immediately.

SERVES 6–8

8–10 boneless chicken thighs, skins on
$\frac{1}{2}$ cup (125 ml) ketjap manis
$\frac{1}{2}$ cup (125 ml) soy sauce
$\frac{1}{2}$ cup (125 ml) Chinese rice wine –
  shao-hsing
$\frac{1}{2}$ cup grated palm sugar
3 teaspoons freshly ground pepper
6 star anise
2 cinnamon sticks
peanut oil

GREENS
4 bunches Chinese greens, blanched,
  dried and halved
1 tablespoon sesame oil
1 tablespoon soy sauce
1 tablespoon water
1 teaspoon white sesame seeds
1 teaspoon black sesame seeds

rosemary skewered lamb with coriander relish

Skewers are a fun thing for the barbecue. They enable the easy turning and handling of food while on the grill and make for equal portioning as well. Choose long, straight, woody rosemary branches, stripping off all the leaves except for a tuft at one end. If there is no time for skewers, marinate the whole steaks and then slice the cooked meat. Another option is to marinate a butterflied leg of lamb to cook whole on the grill. I'd serve these kebabs with the grilled yoghurt bread on page 74.

strip the leaves from the rosemary branches to within 5 cm (2") of the end and soak in water for 20 minutes.

Place the cubed lamb in a shallow ceramic or stainless steel dish.

Combine the marinade ingredients in a bowl and pour over the lamb. Cover and leave to marinate in the fridge for up to 24 hours.

Place all the relish ingredients in a food processor and blend until you have a smooth green sauce.

Preheat the barbecue.

Thread the lamb onto rosemary branches or skewers and grill until the meat is well coloured on the outside and still pink but not raw inside.

Pile onto a platter and serve the coriander relish in a bowl.

SERVES 6–8

12–16 straight rosemary branches, or skewers

1 kg (2 lb 2 oz) boneless lamb steaks, cubed 2.5 cm (1")

MARINADE
juice 2 limes
1 large red onion, chopped
3 cloves garlic, finely chopped
1 teaspoon coriander seeds, toasted and ground (page 197)
1 teaspoon cumin seeds, toasted and ground
1 tablespoon olive oil
handful fresh mint leaves, finely chopped
1 tablespoon well flavoured honey
2 teaspoons salt

RELISH
1 large bunch coriander, leaves picked and chopped
8 tablespoons thick, Greek-style yoghurt
juice 2 limes
zest 1 lime
2 green chillies, seeded and finely chopped
salt

charcutiers hamburgers

Homemade hamburgers are quite a treat these days. The flavour of these gourmet burgers, from one of Ray McVinnie's classes, most definitely benefit from being given time to marinate. Serve with or without the obligatory bun.

combine all the ingredients, mixing well. Cover and refrigerate for as long as possible, preferably overnight.

Preheat the barbecue and spray or brush well with oil. Form the mixture into small, flat patties.

Grill over a medium heat until the outside is brown and the hamburgers are cooked through (the juices must run clear).

Serve with gherkins and wholegrain mustard or your favourite sauce.

MAKES APPROXIMATELY 16

500 g (1 lb) minced topside beef

100 g (4 oz) streaky bacon, finely chopped

250 g (9 oz) chicken livers, cleaned

1 small onion, finely chopped

4 cloves garlic, finely chopped

$1\frac{1}{2}$ tablespoons thyme, chopped

1 tablespoon coriander seeds, toasted and bruised

3 tablespoons port or sherry

3 tablespoons red wine

1 tablespoon sugar

sea salt and freshly ground pepper

lamb and shallot kebabs with pomegranate molasses dressing

Pomegranate molasses is one of the 'new' ingredients – to us that is. It's been around a very long time in the Eastern Mediterranean. It is the concentrated and caramelised juice from the fruit of the same name and has a most irresistible sweet/sour taste. This dish was a favourite when we cooked it in class. Serve the lamb and the shallots tucked into or wrapped in pita breads, which have also been grilled, for just a second each side, on the hotplate of the barbecue.

combine the lamb mince, garlic, salt, pepper and cumin until thoroughly blended. Set aside.

Blanch the shallots in boiling water for 2–3 minutes then plunge into cold water. Peel and trim.

Thread 3 shallots onto each of 6 skewers leaving a 3 cm (1¼") space between each one. Lightly wet your hands and, taking a portion of the meat about equal in size to the shallots, mould around the skewer, squeezing gently into a flattened shape. Repeat, forming 3 portions of meat per skewer. Cook immediately or refrigerate until needed.

Combine all the dressing ingredients in a large bowl and whisk.

Heat the barbecue to a medium temperature and oil well. Grill the kebabs until the lamb is just done – 4–5 minutes each side.

Remove the kebabs from the heat and, using a fork, slide the meat and shallots off the skewers and into a bowl of dressing. Toss to coat and let stand for up to 5 minutes, allowing the flavours to be absorbed by the meat.

SERVES 6

KEBABS

500 g (1 lb) lamb mince
2 garlic cloves, crushed
1 teaspoon salt
½ teaspoon freshly ground pepper
1 teaspoon ground, toasted cumin
18 shallots, blanched
pita breads to serve
6 wooden skewers, soaked

DRESSING

2 tablespoons pomegranate molasses
1 tablespoon lemon juice
zest of 1 lemon, finely chopped
1 garlic clove, finely chopped
1 teaspoon honey
1–2 tablespoons extra virgin olive oil
½ teaspoon sea salt
2–3 tablespoons chopped mint
**2–3 tablespoons chopped flatleaf
   parsley**

warm grilled potato salad with cured olives and parmigiano reggiano

Early in 1999 we moved the Epicurean to a new location and to celebrate the first term in our new school we invited several overseas chefs to visit. Among our impressive lineup was Joanne Weir, a well known American cook, whose food is fresh and seasonal. This is a delicious but simple way to serve potatoes.

preheat the oven to 190°C/375°F.

Wash the potatoes and place in a single layer in a shallow roasting pan. Drizzle with 1 tablespoon of olive oil, season with salt and pepper, cover with foil and bake until tender – 50 to 60 minutes.

Preheat the barbecue or ridged grill.

Cut the potatoes in half and place in a bowl. Drizzle with 2 tablespoons of olive oil and grill, turning occasionally, until hot and golden – 5 to 7 minutes. Remove from the grill and place in a large serving bowl. Add the remaining 2 tablespoons of olive oil, spring onions, garlic, parsley, oregano and olives. Season to taste with salt and pepper.

Using a cheese shaver, shave long thin pieces of Parmigiano Reggiano onto the top of the potatoes. Toss gently and serve immediately.

SERVES 6

1 kg (2 lb 2 oz) small red-skinned new
*   potatoes*
5 tablespoons extra virgin olive oil
sea salt and freshly ground pepper
5 spring onions, white and green,
*   thinly sliced*
2 cloves garlic, crushed
2 tablespoons fresh, coarsely chopped
*   flatleaf parsley*
2 teaspoons fresh chopped oregano
½ cup cured black olives, pitted
85 g (3 oz) piece Parmigiano
*   Reggiano*

honey mustard coleslaw

There are many, many versions of this classic salad, some good and some not so good. This is one of the good ones. Honey mustard is an interesting condiment usually available in delicatessens. It's a great alternative to regular mustard with ham off the bone. It is possible to improvise with hot mustard and a well flavoured honey, such as our lovely manuka.

slice the cabbage as finely as possible. Cover with iced water and leave for 1 hour.

Mix together the mayonnaise, honey mustard, sour cream, cider vinegar and caraway seeds.

Drain the cabbage well, removing as much water as possible. Toss with the dressing.

Cover and chill in the fridge, then toss again before serving.

SERVES 6

$^1/_2$ **small green cabbage**
$^1/_2$ **small red cabbage**
1 cup homemade mayonnaise (page 194)
2 tablespoons honey mustard
$^1/_2$ **cup sour cream**
2–4 tablespoons cider vinegar
1 teaspoon caraway seeds

almond cake with grilled peaches and basil syrup

Believe it or not, this cake has a barbecue component too. This is just one of Ray McVinnie's 'barbecued' desserts. There are lots of variations you can try, such as plums, nectarines or even beautifully ripe well coloured apricots. If you don't feel like grilling the fruit, soak the cake with a lemon syrup and serve with a fresh fruit salad or with fruit steeped in sweet wine.

preheat the oven to 180°C/350°F. Grease a 24 cm/10" cake tin with butter and line the base with baking paper.

Cream the egg yolks, sugar and zest in an electric mixer until pale and thick. Whisk the egg whites until stiff but not dry. With a large spoon, fold a quarter of the beaten whites into the egg yolk mixture and then gently fold through the balance. Stir in the almonds. Pour into the prepared cake tin and bake for 45 minutes.

While the cake is baking make the syrup. Combine the syrup ingredients in a saucepan and bring to the boil. Boil for 2 minutes, then cool and strain out the basil.

Leaving the cake in its tin, pour half the syrup over the hot cake. Let the cake cool. Chill the other half of the syrup.

Preheat the barbecue and make sure the hotplate is very clean.

Cut each peach half into 4. Lightly brush with olive oil and grill until browned, but not collapsing.

Remove the cooled cake from the tin and peel off the baking paper. Place on a serving dish. Pile the grilled peaches on top and just before serving pour the remaining syrup over the top and dust with icing sugar. Garnish with basil leaves and serve with clotted cream.

SERVES 8–10

CAKE
6 large eggs, separated
225 g (8 oz) caster sugar
zest of 1 lemon
250 g (9 oz) finely ground blanched almonds

SYRUP
2 cups sugar
$\frac{1}{2}$ cup (125 ml) water
1$\frac{1}{2}$ cups basil leaves and stalks, loosely packed, save some perfect leaves for garnish

6 large peaches, peeled, halved and stoned
olive oil
clotted cream to serve

elegant lunch

A weekday lunch at home for friends or business colleagues should be more relaxing than a restaurant but it still requires light, elegant food that does not leave everyone needing an afternoon nap. This is generally not a lingering lunch so dishes need to be small and easy to serve quickly without the need for long gaps between courses. Dessert could be replaced with cheese and fruit – perhaps a single cheese with quince paste or a beautiful pear.

curried asparagus soup with cream

Chilled soups are rarely served during hot weather these days, except perhaps the classic Spanish gazpacho. This creamy asparagus soup, subtly flavoured with curry spices, is good served hot or cold.

cut the tips off the asparagus and blanch these in boiling water until just tender. Drain and refresh in cold water. Set aside.

Chop the rest of the asparagus.

Heat the butter in a large saucepan. Add the onion, ginger and curry powder and cook gently until the onions wilt. Add the stock and chopped asparagus and bring to the boil. Cover, reduce the heat to a simmer and cook for 30 minutes. Purée the mixture in a blender until smooth.

Return to a clean saucepan and reheat gently. Stir in the cream and milk and season to taste. Serve hot or chilled, garnished with the reserved asparagus tips and a swirl of cream.

SERVES 4–6

500 g (1 lb) asparagus spears
1/4 cup (60 g) unsalted butter
1 large onion, sliced
1 tablespoon fresh ginger, coarsely chopped
1 1/2 teaspoons curry powder, curry paste or garam masala
1 litre (4 cups) chicken stock
1 cup (250 ml) cream
1/2 cup (125 ml) milk
sea salt and freshly ground pepper
extra cream to garnish

rock oysters with ginger soy sambal

For oyster aficionados rock oysters served this way are irresistible. Keep the oysters chilled and spoon over the sauce just before serving. A good way to keep the shells firmly positioned is to make a bed of salt on which to sit them.

Laurie Black prepared these oysters two ways in a class entitled 'Reality Bites'.

carefully slice the ginger into very fine julienne.

Cut the chillies and spring onion straight across into thin rings.

Gently stir together the ginger, chillies, spring onion, lemon zest and juice, coriander and soy sauce. Let the sambal sit for 30 minutes.

Arrange the oysters in their shells on a platter and spoon a little sambal onto each.

5 cm (2") piece ginger, peeled
2 fresh long red chillies
1 spring onion
zest and juice of 1 lemon
1 tablespoon chopped coriander stalk
4 tablespoons Japanese soy sauce
2 dozen rock oysters, loosened from the shell, any grit removed

oysters with lime and sesame

To me, Bluff oysters are the 'Rolls-Royce' of all oysters and the best way to eat them is the simplest – lightly buttered brown bread with a squeeze of lemon and a grind of pepper. The only other essential is a fork or toothpick, depending whether or not you're in company, to transfer each oyster to the bread. However, I am open to new ideas and this one is definitely worth trying.

whisk together the lime juice, sesame oil and daikon. Season with salt and pepper and stir in the sesame seeds.

Arrange the oysters on shells or spoons. Spoon over the sauce.

4 tablespoons fresh lime juice
2 tablespoons sesame oil
1 tablespoon finely grated daikon radish
sea salt and freshly ground black pepper
1 teaspoon toasted sesame seeds
2 dozen oysters, removed from the shell

Rock Oysters with Ginger Soy Sambal (left) and Oysters with Lime and Sesame (right)

asparagus and pesto soufflé

The asparagus season is a relatively short one so we need to make the most of it. Although we mostly eat asparagus steamed with a drizzle of butter or olive oil and a squeeze of lemon, there are many other ways to prepare it. This dish can be made as one or, for a more elegant presentation, as four individual soufflés.

preheat the oven to 180°C/350°F.

Brush a baking dish or heat-proof platter with the melted butter. Dust with the Parmesan cheese and tap the dish to distribute the cheese evenly.

Melt the butter over a low heat in a medium saucepan. Add the flour and whisk for 2 minutes until the mixture starts to bubble. Add the cream and whisk over a low heat until thickened.

Add the pesto, salt, pepper and ½ cup of the Parmesan cheese. Allow the mixture to cool, then beat in the egg yolks one at a time. Set aside to cool.

Whisk the egg whites with a pinch of salt until stiff. Carefully fold the beaten whites into the cooled cheese mixture.

Place the blanched asparagus on the prepared platter. Sprinkle with sliced roasted capsicum. Spoon the soufflé mix on top of the vegetables, covering completely. Sprinkle with the remaining cheese.

Bake for 25–35 minutes or until puffed and browned. If the top browns too quickly, cover with foil for the remaining cooking time. Serve immediately.

SERVES 4

2 tablespoons unsalted butter, melted
2 tablespoons grated Parmesan cheese

3 tablespoons unsalted butter
3 tablespoons flour
1½ cups (375 ml) cream
1½ tablespoons pesto
sea salt and freshly ground pepper
1 cup freshly grated Parmesan cheese
3 egg yolks
5 egg whites

500 g (1 lb) asparagus, briefly blanched, drained and dried well
1 red capsicum, roasted and peeled, sliced

94

cured beef with goats cheese and celeriac salad

This is a delightful dish which Clare Ferguson adapted from one she ate at London's Zefferano Restaurant. Any Italian cured meat can be used – Bresaola or Prosciutto for instance. Whereas celery is available all year round, celeriac is less common. If you do find it, it is also very good braised.

slice the celeriac or celery into thin, match-like julienne. Put in a bowl, cover with boiling water and let stand for 1 minute. Drain and refresh in ice water. Drain again and dry on kitchen paper.

Crumble the cheese and use a fork to mash it with the oil and wine into a creamy dressing. Add the celeriac or celery and toss well.

Cover 4 plates with overlapping slices of cured meat. Divide the salad mixture between, piling it into mounds in the centre. Sprinkle with parsley, sea salt and pepper, and finish with a drizzle of truffle oil.

SERVES 4

*100 g (4 oz) celeriac or 2–4 celery
    stalks*
50 g (2 oz) crumbly goats cheese
2 tablespoons extra virgin olive oil
2 tablespoons dry white wine
*20 very thin slices of cured beef or
    other cured meat or salami*
Italian parsley
sea salt and freshly ground pepper
truffle oil or lemon infused olive oil

goats cheese on salad leaves with anchovy dressing

Stephanie Alexander has visited our school twice. On her second visit, in 1996, she launched her bible,
The Cook's Companion, *in New Zealand at the Epicurean. This dish is one she prepared for her classes
at that time and it's one I have made often since, using our Saratoga Dairy Gladstone Chevre. Serve it as
an entrée or a luncheon dish.*

brush the slices of bread with 1 tablespoon of the oil. Bake or grill quickly until golden on both sides, then wipe with a cut garlic clove. Set aside.

Melt half the butter, cool and whisk together with the egg. Roll each slice of goats cheese in the mixture. Press a generous layer of breadcrumbs onto each slice of cheese and refrigerate until needed.

Place the anchovies in a small bowl resting over a saucepan of simmering water. The anchovies will melt into a cream. Remove and keep aside.

When ready to serve, divide the salad leaves between 4 plates. Divide the croutons between the salads. Heat the remaining butter in a non-stick pan and cook the cheeses on both sides until golden, turning very gently with a spatula. Carefully place the cheeses onto the salad leaves. Finely chop the remaining clove of garlic and add to the frying pan. Sauté for 1 minute. Stir in the anchovies, the remaining oil and the chopped herbs. Remove at once and spoon over the salad leaves and cheese. Grind pepper over and serve.

SERVES 4

8 slices sourdough bread stick or good French bread
4 tablespoons extra virgin olive oil
2 cloves garlic
80 g (3 oz) butter
1 egg
8 slices fresh goats cheese
1 cup fine toasted breadcrumbs
2 anchovies, finely chopped
2 cups small salad leaves, washed and dried
2 tablespoons freshly chopped parsley
2 teaspoons freshly chopped chives
freshly ground black pepper

scallops with spinach leaves and verjuice sauce

Butter sauces are more of a treat than an everyday occurrence and for good reason. This simple dish was made by Maggie Beer, on her visit to Epicurean in 1995, using verjuice, one of the products Maggie produces under her own name in the Barossa Valley in South Australia. Verjuice is a gentle acidulant and this is just one of its many uses (see page 197). I cook this dish only when New Zealand scallops are in season.

heat a frying pan over a low heat, melt 30 g (1 oz) of the butter and cook gently until it is a light brown colour. Place the spinach in the pan with salt, pepper and nutmeg, stir well and remove to drain on paper towels.

Heat the oil with the remaining butter, season the scallops with salt and pepper and sear in the pan for about 1 minute on each side. Remove to a plate.

Reduce the shallots and verjuice with a little salt until syrupy. Gradually whisk in the butter, maintaining the heat right through, but do not allow to boil. Season with lemon juice, salt and pepper to taste. Set aside in a warm place until needed to sauce the scallops.

Divide the spinach between 6 plates and place 6 scallops on top. Spoon over the sauce and garnish with a few sprigs of chervil and lemon wedges.

SERVES 6

50 g (2 oz) unsalted butter
250 g (9 oz) small spinach leaves, deveined, washed and dried well
sea salt and freshly ground pepper
freshly grated nutmeg
2 teaspoons olive oil
36 fresh scallops with their coral, cleaned

SAUCE
4 shallots, sliced thinly
1 cup verjuice
salt and freshly ground pepper
250 g (9 oz) chilled unsalted butter, cubed
juice of 1 lemon

chervil
lemon wedges

snapper baked 'en papillote' with spaghettini, rocket and chilli oil

Some years ago, Dietmar Sawyere made a name for himself as executive chef of the Hyatt Hotel in Auckland. Returning from Sydney recently, he established Number Five City Road, now one of my favourite restaurants. We are doubly fortunate because when he teaches at Epicurean he generously shares many of the dishes on his menu.

Have these parcels prepared ahead, ready to cook at the last moment. The shiitake and enoki mushrooms are grown commercially in this country and should be easy to find.

preheat the oven to 200°C/400°F.

Cut out 6 large heart-shaped pieces of baking paper and place on the bench.

In a bowl toss the spaghettini with the chilli oil and season well.

Divide the pasta between the 6 papers, placing it on one half of the paper.

Place the shiitake and rocket leaves on top of the pasta. Season.

Place the snapper, skin-side up, on top of the rocket. Season.

Top the fish with the enoki and 2 slices of chilli and sprinkle with lemon juice. Cut the log of garlic butter into 6 and place one slice on top of each fillet.

Fold over the other side of the heart shape and, starting at the wide end, fold over the edges of the parcel thereby sealing the parcel tightly.

Bake in a hot oven for 10 minutes. Serve in the bag, unopened, with a wedge of lemon and a sprig of chervil on the side. Each guest can then tear open their parcel and enjoy the aromas as they escape.

SERVES 6

baking paper

140 g (5 oz) spaghettini, cooked

2 teaspoons chilli oil

100 g (4 oz) fresh shiitake mushrooms, sliced

handful rocket leaves

sea salt and white pepper

6 x 120 g (4$\frac{1}{2}$ oz) snapper fillets, skin on (baby snapper if possible)

20 g ($\frac{3}{4}$ oz) enoki mushrooms, trimmed to 4 cm (1$\frac{1}{2}$") lengths

12 slices red chilli

1 lemon

6 tablespoons garlic butter, in a log

6 lemon wedges

6 sprigs chervil

oven baked salmon with courgette and wasabi potato cake

Salmon is a good fish to serve when entertaining. Not only does it always look pretty on the plate, but it's also easy to cook. When Simon Gault cooked this dish for us, he used fresh wasabi, grated in the potato cakes, so if you can find this by all means use it instead of the paste. You will need about 2 tablespoons. These cakes are also good to serve with other meats.

preheat the oven to 220°C/425°F.

Butter 4 ramekins, about 100 ml (3½ oz) each.

Melt the butter in a pan and sauté the courgette, potato and shallot for about 4 minutes. Add the wasabi paste and stir to combine. Pack tightly into the ramekins and place them in a roasting pan. Fill the pan with boiling water to halfway up the sides of the ramekins. Bake for 30 minutes. Run a knife around the edge of the cake and turn out onto plates.

Meanwhile, sauté the shallot for the sauce in the teaspoon of butter in a small pan. Add the vinegars, bring to the boil and reduce by two thirds. Add the cream, bring to the boil again, then reduce the heat. Whisk in the chilled butter piece by piece until the sauce is emulsified and thick. Season and set aside.

Season the salmon fillets with salt and pepper and place on a buttered tray. Bake for about 7 minutes until the fish is warmed through but still rare in the centre.

Place a piece of salmon on top of each potato cake and spoon over the sauce. Garnish with a fresh herb and lemon wedges.

SERVES 4

POTATO CAKE

2 teaspoons butter

320 g (11 oz) courgette, grated

170 g (6 oz) potato, grated

1 shallot, finely chopped

1 teaspoon wasabi paste

SAUCE

½ shallot, finely chopped

1 teaspoon butter, extra

6 tablespoons white wine vinegar

1 tablespoon balsamic vinegar

3 tablespoons cream

120 g (4½ oz) butter, finely diced and chilled

sea salt and freshly ground pepper

4 x 170 g (6 oz) salmon fillets

fresh herbs and lemon wedges to garnish

coffee toffee ice cream

With the advent of small, inexpensive ice-cream machines, it is now possible to make very good ice-cream at home. Several things go into making the perfect ice-cream. Fat, usually in the form of eggs yolks and cream, is important for a creamy texture and taste – not enough and the ice-cream will taste 'thin'. Also important is churning, which acts to prohibit the formation of ice crystals, and the addition of sugar or alcohol, which will inhibit freezing and produce a softer result.

toffee

line a baking tray with a non-stick baking sheet or baking paper and set aside.

Combine the sugar and water in a heavy-based saucepan and heat to dissolve the sugar, then bring to the boil and simmer until amber in colour. Do not allow to become too dark. Whisk in the butter and when it is well mixed pour into the prepared tray. Set aside to cool and when hard break into pieces. Keep aside a piece measuring roughly 15 x 15 cm (6" x 6"), and process the rest in a food processor until finely chopped. Chop the reserved piece roughly with a knife. Store in an airtight container.

ice-cream

heat the cream in a saucepan over a high heat until just below the boil. Beat the egg yolks in a heat-proof bowl until creamy, then slowly beat in the hot cream. Add the sugar.

Place the bowl over a saucepan of simmering water and cook until the mixture coats the back of a wooden spoon. Mix in the coffee, cover immediately and chill.

When chilled, churn the mixture in an ice-cream machine until frozen, then fold in the crushed toffee and transfer to a container. Store in the freezer.

Alternatively, if an ice-cream machine is not available, freeze the mixture until firm, then process in a food processor, or beat with an electric mixer, until the consistency is creamy.

Fold in the toffee and freeze again until solid.

To serve, place 2–3 small scoops in an espresso cup, sprinkle with roughly chopped toffee and place a few amaretti biscuits on the side.

TOFFEE

1 cup sugar

4 tablespoons water

45 g (1$\frac{1}{2}$ oz) unsalted butter

ICE CREAM

2 cups (500 ml) cream

6 large egg yolks

500 g (1 lb) sugar

2 cups (500 ml) very strong, freshly brewed coffee

SERVES 8

lemon pots of cream

Sometimes after a lunch it's nice to serve something more than fruit, but nothing rich or heavy. This silky, baked lemon custard is perfect served in very little cups or ramekins with a tiny biscuit. Remember not to overcook them.

preheat the oven to 170°C/325°F.

Whisk the eggs, yolks and sugar together in the bowl of an electric mixer until thick.

Add the lemon juice, then the cream. Strain through a fine sieve and then add the lemon zest.

Pour the mixture into 12 x 190 ml (7 oz) custard cups or ramekins. Place them in a roasting pan and add enough boiling water to come halfway up the sides of the cups. Cover the pan loosely with foil and bake until the custards are just set – 40–45 minutes. The custard should still be soft in the centre when lightly shaken. Remove from the pan and cool. Serve warm or cold with a crisp biscuit.

SERVES 12

2 eggs

8 egg yolks

$1\frac{1}{4}$–$1\frac{1}{2}$ cups caster sugar

1 cup (250 ml) lemon juice

$2\frac{1}{2}$ cups (625 ml) cream

zest of 1 lemon

a summer buffet

'Buffet' is one of those rather old-fashioned words that has hung around, despite us having a more modern approach to the concept these days. It is certainly an easy process to allow guests to help themselves to food, and buffets can be less labour intensive for the host, encouraging social mingling and a less formal atmosphere. One of the less desirable effects is that guests pile their plates with a littlebit of everything and end up with a hapless mix of flavours that normally would not be found on one plate. So, as I often preach, less is best. Even though you may wish to cater for everyone's varied tastes and needs, it is possible to do so with a series of dishes which, when combined, creates harmony, not hell.

Balance is also important. On a buffet you need meat, fish or poultry, vegetables, bread and salad. Food should be seasonal, and there should be variety in colour and texture, as well as hot and cold dishes. Think, too, about practical aspects such as not having chilli in every dish or mayonnaise on every salad, and some things can be prepared ahead and just be dressed at the last minute.

asparagus with anchovy cream

Asparagus is one of life's pleasures and a seasonal one that we anticipate each year. Blanched asparagus, still with a bit of a bite and by now a brilliant green, looks magnificent on a platter all on its own. Simply have an interesting sauce to dip into or spoon over. There are plenty of theories as to the best way to cook asparagus. My advice, either use a tall specially designed pot with a basket which sees the thick ends in the water and the tips just steaming, or lie it all in a wide shallow pan and watch like a hawk to prevent overcooking the tips. Julie le Clerc prepared aparagus this way in one of our 'Come for Cocktails' classes.

blanch the asparagus in boiling, salted water until just cooked. Drain and immediately plunge into iced water until thoroughly cold. Drain and dry.

Place the yolks, garlic, mustard and lemon juice in a bowl of the food processor. Process until pale and creamy. With the motor running, add the oil in a thin and steady stream. Add the anchovies to taste and process until incorporated. Adjust the seasoning and add extra lemon juice if more acidity is desired.

MAKES 2 CUPS

asparagus spears, trimmed

ANCHOVY CREAM
3 egg yolks
2 cloves garlic, peeled
1 tablespoon Dijon mustard
juice of 1 lemon
$1\frac{1}{4}$ cups (375 ml) vegetable oil
6–10 anchovies
salt and pepper

charred red capsicums filled with couscous in a cumin vinaigrette

This colourful dish would look wonderful alongside the asparagus on any buffet. The secret here is to char the capsicums over a flame, rather than in the oven. They need to retain some body to be strong enough to hold the couscous and sit nicely on a plate.

combine the lemon juice, vinegar, garlic and cumin in a bowl and slowly add the oil, whisking constantly until smooth and creamy. Season with salt and pepper.

Heat the oil in a large saucepan over a medium heat. Add the spring onion, red capsicum and courgettes and cook, covered, for 5 minutes or until tender. Add the couscous and stock and season with salt and pepper. Bring to the boil, cover tightly and immediately remove from the heat. Set aside for 10 minutes. Pour the vinaigrette over the couscous, add the parsley and adjust the seasoning. Toss gently with a fork and let marinate for an hour.

To serve, take a sharp knife and carefully cut a circle around the stem of each roasted pepper. Remove and discard the stems and carefully remove all the seeds with a small spoon, keeping the peppers whole. Fill the peppers with the couscous and serve at room temperature.

SERVES 6

VINAIGRETTE
juice of a lemon
1 tablespoon sherry vinegar
1 large clove garlic, mashed
$\frac{1}{2}$ teaspoon cumin seeds, toasted and crushed
6–8 tablespoons olive oil
sea salt and freshly ground pepper

COUSCOUS
2 tablespoons olive oil
$\frac{1}{2}$ cup finely chopped spring onions
$\frac{1}{2}$ cup finely chopped red capsicums
$\frac{1}{2}$ cup finely chopped courgettes
1 cup instant couscous
2 cups (500 ml) chicken stock
sea salt and freshly ground pepper
3 tablespoons parsley, finely chopped

6 charred, red capsicums, peeled and left whole (see page 196)

pan bagna

Years ago, at my old delicatessen, La Moutardière, we made Pan Bagna every weekend in the summer. These loaves, with the centres removed, were packed full of cured meats, cheese, vegetables and fresh herbs, weighted and then sliced. This is peasant food at its best – they knew what they were doing when they took their lunch to the fields each day packed into hollowed out loaves. The filling ingredients here are merely our favorites. There are many other options – roasted eggplant and courgettes, feta cheese, capers, salami, prosciutto – the list could go on. The only essential – really good bread with a crust that will hold up well under the pressure.

cut the baguette in half lengthways and scoop out a little of the bread down the centre of each half. Mix together the olive oil, red wine vinegar and garlic and season with salt and pepper. Brush both sides of the baguette generously. Spread the tomato on the bottom half of the bread, then lay on the whole anchovies. Cover with a layer of basil leaves followed by artichoke bottoms, then cheese. Sprinkle on the black olives then finish with a layer of roasted red capsicum. Cover with the top half of the baguette.

Press together and wrap tightly in plastic wrap or tinfoil. Refrigerate, with a weight on top, long enough for the juices and oils to be well absorbed – a minimum of 1 hour or up to 24 hours.

To serve, cut into slices.

SERVES 4–6

1 sourdough baguette

5 tablespoons extra virgin olive oil

2 tablespoons red wine vinegar

1 garlic clove, crushed

sea salt and freshly ground pepper

2 firm tomatoes, deseeded and chopped

4-6 anchovies

basil leaves

4 artichoke hearts or bottoms, chopped

100 g (4 oz) semi-soft cheese – provolone, gruyere or mozzarella, sliced

8 black olives, stoned and chopped

2 red capsicums, roasted and peeled (see page 196)

mussels with lemon salad

Every buffet should have at least one seafood or fish dish. This is a very pretty dish and an easy one to serve from a platter. Serve at room temperature.

to make the salad, remove the segments of lemon flesh from between each membrane and finely chop. Chop the onion to the same size. Mix all the ingredients together in a bowl, cover and chill.

Purée the coriander leaves, garlic and salt and pepper with a hand-held blender or small food processor, gradually adding sufficient olive oil to form a smooth, bright green sauce. Cover and set aside.

Heat a little water or white wine in a large pan. Add the mussels, cover and steam, removing them as they open. Ladle the sauce onto a platter, place the mussels on top and spoon some lemon salad to one side. Garnish with a few coriander leaves.

SERVES 6–8

SALAD

4 large lemons, peeled of all pith
1 large onion
1/2 preserved lemon, rind only, finely chopped (see glossary page 195)
sea salt

SAUCE

1 bunch coriander, leaves picked
1 clove garlic, peeled
sea salt and freshly ground pepper
olive oil

MUSSELS

water or white wine
24–30 green-lipped mussels in the shell, scrubbed
extra coriander leaves to garnish

tuna tonnato

The traditional Italian dish Veal Tonnato inspired this version using fresh tuna steaks. As always with fresh tuna, it's essential to keep it rare, so it will be tender and succulent. Serve at room temperature.

brush the tuna steaks with olive oil and set aside.

Heat a little olive oil and fry the capers until crisp – they will open out like little flowers. Drain on paper towels and set aside.

For the sauce, blend the tuna, capers and anchovies to a smooth paste in a food processor, then add the mayonnaise. If the sauce is thicker than cream, thin with a little water or lemon juice. Season to taste with sea salt and pepper.

Grill or barbecue the tuna until it is still pink in the centre. Place on a platter and coat with tonnato sauce and crispy fried capers to garnish.

SERVES 6

6 x 150 g (5 oz) tuna steaks
olive oil
capers

TONNATO SAUCE
150 g (5 oz) tuna in olive oil, drained
1 tablespoon capers, drained
4 anchovies
1$\frac{1}{2}$ cups (375 ml) homemade
  mayonnaise (see page 194)
lemon juice to taste
sea salt and freshly ground white
  pepper

sicilian salad with roasted eggplant, capsicums and garlic

The flavours in this salad are simply delicious! Serve it alongside a platter of cold lamb, cooked rare on the barbecue. The little Japanese eggplants are readily available much of the year, but should they prove elusive, just use any variety you can find.

preheat the oven to 250°C/500°F.

Cut the capsicums in half and remove the stems, seeds and membrane. Place on a lightly oiled baking sheet cut-side down and brush liberally with olive oil. Roast until their skins begin to blister and darken – about 15 minutes. Remove from the oven and place in a covered bowl to steam.

Lower the oven to 190°C/375°F. Toss the unpeeled garlic cloves in a little oil and slice the eggplant into thick slices (2 cm/ ¾″) and toss in the remaining oil and the chopped garlic, salt and pepper. Place the garlic and eggplant on an oiled baking tray and roast until the garlic is soft and the eggplant tender – 12–15 minutes. Remove from the oven and set aside to cool.

Peel the capsicums and cut into 1.75 cm (½″) strips, saving the juices for the salad. Slice the eggplant into similar strips and peel the garlic, removing the stem end.

Combine the vegetables and toss with balsamic vinegar. Add a splash of white wine vinegar and season well. Allow to marinate for an hour at room temperature.

Arrange the watercress on a platter and spoon the salad on top. Garnish with olives and serve at room temperature.

SERVES 4–6

2 medium red or yellow capsicums
1 tablespoon extra virgin olive oil
16 cloves garlic, unpeeled
1 kg (2 lb 2 oz) Japanese eggplants
2 cloves garlic, finely chopped
sea salt and freshly ground pepper
2 tablespoons balsamic vinegar
white wine vinegar
2 cups watercress sprigs
12 black olives

mushrooms with mint and tomato

Include these mushrooms on an antipasti platter or serve them as a vegetable dish. The roasted tomato adds a real depth to the dish, but if time is of the essence use a fresh ripe tomato.

wipe the mushrooms with a damp cloth to remove any dirt and trim the stems.

Heat the olive oil in large skillet. Add the mushrooms and garlic and toss in the oil. Cover and cook over a medium heat for 2–4 minutes, or until just cooked. Add the tomato and cook for another minute. Remove from the heat, add the lemon juice, vinegar, mint and cayenne and season to taste.

Allow to cool before serving.

SERVES 4 AS A VEGETABLE

500 g (1 lb) medium-sized flat mushrooms
6 tablespoons olive oil
2 large cloves garlic, thinly sliced
1 large roasted tomato, peeled, seeded and diced
3 tablespoons lemon juice
2 teaspoons red wine vinegar
1 tablespoon mint leaves, finely chopped
pinch cayenne
sea salt and freshly ground pepper

mediterranean onions

Over the last few years we've all become familiar with onions which have been slow cooked to become 'marmalade'. This dish uses the same technique of slow cooking which caramelises the sugars in the onions. The result is rich and buttery and quite irresistible.

preheat the oven to 150°C/300°F.

Trim one end off each onion and discard. Leave the skin on and slice into 1.5 cm (½") slices. Discard the other end.

Cover a baking tray with a teflon baking sheet. Place the slices on the sheet and brush lightly with olive oil. Bake at least an hour, turning with a spatula halfway through. The onions should be caramelised – discard any burnt bits.

Using a spatula, transfer the slices to a wide, shallow serving dish. Remove the skins as you do so and any dried outer rings. Mix the remaining oil with the garlic, chilli, parsley, vinegar and water. Season with salt and pepper.

Spoon the dressing over the onions and serve at room temperature.

SERVES 6

5 large brown onions – about 1 kg
5 tablespoons olive oil
1 clove garlic, finely chopped
¼ teaspoon red chilli flakes or 1 small red chilli, seeded and chopped
1 tablespoon chopped parsley
1 teaspoon red wine vinegar
2 tablespoons water
sea salt and freshly ground pepper

115

ginger beef with japanese eggplant and green beans

I've put this dish in the buffet chapter, but it could fit equally well into the barbecue one. In fact, Ray McVinnie cooked this in one of his famous barbecue classes. Either serve it straight away while still warm or cook all the components ahead, assembling the dish just before serving at room temperature. Eye fillet is the preferred cut, but rump, sirloin or scotch fillet are also suitable. To extract the juice from ginger, grate and then collect all the ginger up in your hand and squeeze. Discard the fibre that remains.

slice the semi-frozen beef very thinly.

Mix the marinade ingredients together until the sugar is dissolved. Pour over the beef and marinate for 1 hour.

Blanch the beans in boiling water for 1 minute, refresh in cold water and drain. Toss lightly in a little sesame oil.

Preheat a ridged grill pan or barbecue hotplate.

Shake excess marinade off the beef and sear quickly on a very hot oiled grill. Brush the eggplant with sesame oil and grill until tender, turning once.

Grill the beans until hot and browned.

Whisk the dressing ingredients together and season to taste with lemon juice and salt and pepper.

Put the eggplant down the middle of a serving platter. Pile the beef on top. Put the beans around the beef. Drizzle the sauce over everything. Sprinkle with spring onion and sesame seeds. Garnish with lemon wedges.

SERVES 4–6

600 g (21 oz) steak in one piece, all fat and sinew removed, partially frozen

MARINADE
5 tablespoons Japanese soy sauce
5 tablespoons sake
5 tablespoons mirin
1 teaspoon sugar
3 tablespoons ginger juice

200 g (7 oz) green beans
sesame oil
4 Japanese eggplants, sliced 1 cm ($\frac{1}{4}$") thick

DRESSING
$\frac{1}{2}$ cup (125 ml) vegetable oil
2 tablespoons Dijon mustard
2 teaspoons rice vinegar
lemon juice to taste
sea salt and freshly ground pepper

2 spring onions, finely sliced on the diagonal
2 tablespoons toasted sesame seeds
lemon wedges

fig and honey syrup cake

At Epicurean, one of the things we most love to do is encourage everyone to cook with the seasons. Fresh figs are still a luxury here and the growing season is all too short. Even if you're lucky enough to have a tree in your garden or access to some of the many wild fig trees, especially in the Far North, you have to be quick to make the most of this beautiful, ancient fruit. Luckily, this cake can be made entirely with dried figs. I'd use the plump round figs rather than the flat, hard ones.

combine the syrup ingredients in a saucepan and dissolve the sugar over a low heat. Bring to the boil and simmer until reduced by about one third. Cool.

Soak the dried figs in the boiling water for 15 minutes then purée in a blender or food processor.

Preheat the oven to 180°C/350°F.

Grease a 24 cm (10") springform tin well and place the fig halves evenly around the tin, cut-side down.

Cream the butter and sugar until fluffy, then beat in the eggs one at a time. Beat in the dried fig purée and vanilla. Add the flour and ground cloves and mix to combine. Spoon the mixture over the figs, smooth the top and cook for 45 minutes or until cooked when tested with a skewer.

Allow to rest for 10 minutes, then turn out of the tin and pour over the cooled syrup. Serve warm with lightly whipped cream.

SERVES 6–8

SYRUP

$\frac{1}{3}$ **cup demerara sugar**

$\frac{1}{3}$ **cup lemon juice**

$\frac{1}{3}$ **cup honey**

CAKE

6 dried figs

$\frac{1}{2}$ **cup boiling water**

6 fresh figs, halved

200 g (7 oz) sugar

200 g (7 oz) unsalted butter

3 large eggs

1 teaspoon vanilla extract

200 g (7 oz) plain flour

$\frac{1}{2}$ **teaspoon ground cloves**

rhubarb and strawberry trifle

On my last birthday, I invited some friends for a barbecue and served this trifle for pudding. Never have I seen so many people queuing for a second helping. What a hit and what a great way to serve these two delicious things. Rhubarb is a highly under-rated 'vegetable'. Both the custard and the fruit can be made up to three days in advance so it's possible to have all the different components ready to assemble just long enough before serving so that the savoiardi have time to soften.

scald the milk and cream by bringing it to just below boiling point over a medium heat.

Beat the egg yolks and sugar until they are thick and pale. Gradually pour the hot milk and cream mixture into the egg and sugar mixture while beating. Add the vanilla. Pour the custard into a heat-proof bowl, place over a saucepan of simmering water and stir constantly until it thickens. The custard is the correct consistency when you can draw your finger across the back of a custard-coated wooden spoon and it leaves a trail.

Cool and chill. This can be made up to three days in advance.

remove the leaves from the rhubarb and discard. Wash the rhubarb and cut into 5 cm (2") pieces. Place in a saucepan with the sugar and cook over a low heat, stirring occasionally, for about 10 minutes or until tender. Add the strawberries and leave to cool.

To assemble, arrange several sponge fingers over the base of a 2 litre (3½ pint), deep, straight-sided serving dish and sprinkle with ¼ of the Marsala. Top with ¼ of the fruit and ¼ of the custard. Continue layering, finishing with a layer of custard, but reserving a large spoonful of fruit. Place this fruit in the centre of the final custard layer, top with the reserved unhulled strawberries and serve with softly whipped cream.

SERVES 6–8

CUSTARD
250 ml (1 cup) milk
250 ml (1 cup) cream
5 large egg yolks
100 g (4 oz) sugar
½ teaspoon vanilla extract

8 stems rhubarb
170 g (6 oz) caster sugar
**1 punnet strawberries, hulled – reserve
   a few unhulled**
**1 packet sponge fingers – savoiardi
   biscuits**
⅓ cup Marsala
1 quantity of custard
extra whipped cream for serving

the cocktail party

One of the traditions that has developed over the years at Epicurean is the annual pre-Christmas class on small bites. By inviting a different guest chef each year to teach this class, we hope to broaden our repertoire of dishes.

A cocktail party can be a great way to return all those invitations in one hit. With good planning, all the hard work can be done ahead, bar a bit of last minute heating and garnishing. Organise a few teenagers to serve the platters of food and trays of drinks, have all the cold food ready to go and serve all the hot items first so you can then relax until everyone leaves.

Variety would have to be one of the key facts to keep in mind. I still feel an acute sense of embarrassment when I remember the first time I organised a cocktail party for one of my father's birthdays. I think I was about 18 at the time. The entire selection of 'small bites' comprised Snax biscuits with a variety of toppings.

smoked chicken rillettes

Rillettes is essentially a French meat paste, traditionally loaded with goose, duck or pork fat. More modern versions manage to lower the fat and still retain the wonderful flavours. Serve rillettes as a spread for croutes or crackers or as a filling for tiny sourdough sandwiches with rocket or watercress. It's good on hot toast too!

bring the stock and wine to the boil in a shallow pan and add the chicken breast and the parsley and thyme sprigs.

Poach, turning once or twice, until the chicken is just cooked. Remove from the poaching liquid and cool.

Take the meat off the smoked chicken, removing any skin at the same time.

Heat the 2 tablespoons of butter in a skillet and add the garlic and smoked chicken meat. Cook for 2–3 minutes, stirring, then remove from the pan and cool.

Place both lots of chicken in the food processor and pulse until the meat is well shredded. Add the softened butter and combine, then season to taste with a little brandy, salt and pepper.

MAKES 3 CUPS

$1\frac{1}{2}$ *cups (375 ml) chicken stock*
$\frac{1}{4}$ *cup white wine*
1 double chicken breast, skin removed
parsley and thyme sprigs
$\frac{1}{2}$ *smoked chicken*
2 tablespoons unsalted butter
1 clove garlic, crushed
100 g (4 oz) unsalted butter, softened
1–2 tablespoons brandy
sea salt and freshly ground pepper

smoked salmon rillettes

place all the ingredients in the food processor and purée to a paste. Taste and season with salt, pepper and lemon juice.

MAKES 2 CUPS

$\frac{3}{4}$ *cup smoked salmon offcuts*
$\frac{1}{2}$ *cup (115 g) unsalted butter, softened*
$\frac{1}{4}$ *cup sour cream*
$\frac{1}{4}$ *cup roasted red capsicum, skin removed and diced (page 196)*
pinch cayenne pepper
sea salt and freshly ground pepper
lemon juice to taste

121

salmon crudo

One of the things I do enjoy about cocktail food is the fact that it's easy to convert favourite dishes into cocktail bites or vice versa. Some small bites can also make great first courses. This salmon dish is a typical example. Serve it on a platter with toothpicks or plate it individually with a few salad leaves and garnish simply with lemon and lime wedges and sprigs of basil. The salmon can be sliced ahead of time ready to be dressed just an hour before serving.

remove the pin bones from the salmon, using tweezers (see glossary). Using a sharp, thin knife, cut the salmon into paper-thin, diagonal pieces.

Place the salmon slices in a single layer on a ceramic dish. At this stage the salmon can be covered well with plastic wrap and refrigerated until an hour before serving. Spoon the lemon and lime juices over the salmon and allow it to marinate in the citrus juices until it 'cooks', i.e., the red flesh of the salmon will turn pink and become opaque in about 2 minutes or so. Refrigerate until ready to serve.

To serve, lift the salmon pieces out of the juices and arrange decoratively on a serving platter. Drizzle the olive oil over the salmon, rubbing it into the fish, then sprinkle with the chopped basil and pepper to taste. Serve with rice crackers or small slices of wholegrain bread.

500 g (1 lb) salmon fillets, skin removed
juice of 2 lemons
juice of 2 limes
1 tablespoon extra virgin olive oil
3 teaspoons fresh basil, finely chopped
freshly ground pepper to taste

mahor

This has to be one of the most moreish combinations ever conceived and our favourite way of serving it is on tiny crisp poppadoms which are sometimes available from Indian or Asian stores. If they can't be found we just cut circles from wonton wrappers and deep fry them in the same way to create boats for the mahor. The mixture can be made well in advance and even freezes well.

half fill the wok with vegetable oil and, when hot, fry the poppadoms in small batches, draining well on paper towels. Then fry the shallots, drain and repeat with the sliced garlic, taking care not to burn them.

Heat a little oil in a frying pan and cook the pork and prawn mince separately. Set aside.

In a small food processor or with a mortar and pestle combine the coriander roots or stalks and unsliced garlic. Grind to a paste.

Using the same pan, fry the paste in a little more oil until light brown then add the palm sugar and caramelise slightly. Add the fish sauce, whiskey, pork and prawns and cook for 10–15 minutes until the mixture resembles jam and will hold together once chilled. Add the peanuts, lime juice to taste and finally the fried garlic and shallots.

Serve chilled or at room temperature on the baby poppadoms, garnished with coriander leaves and a squeeze of lime.

MAKES APPROXIMATELY 4 CUPS

vegetable oil
baby poppadoms (4 cm or 1$\frac{1}{2}$"
*   diameter)*
100 g (4 oz) sliced shallots
100 g (4 oz) sliced garlic
250 g (9 oz) pork mince
250 g (9 oz) prawn meat, minced
50 g (2 oz) coriander root or stalks
50 g (2 oz) garlic
250 g (9 oz) palm sugar, or to taste
*   (see glossary, page 194)*
100 ml (3$\frac{1}{2}$ fl oz) fish sauce
2 tablespoons bourbon whiskey
$\frac{1}{2}$ cup roasted peanuts, chopped
juice of 1 lime
coriander leaves and lime juice to
*   serve*

dolce latte biscuits

For blue cheese fans these little melt in the mouth biscuits are an irresistible accompaniment with a drink. We make such extraordinary blue cheeses in New Zealand that I usually forgo the real Dolce Latte and choose one of ours instead.

place the flour in a bowl of the food processor, add the butter and process until the mixture resembles fine breadcrumbs. Season with a pinch of freshly ground black pepper.

Add the blue cheese and process until the mixture comes together. Turn out onto the bench and knead to a smooth dough. Chill in the refrigerator for about 1 hour, or until the dough is firm and easy to handle.

Preheat the oven to 200°C/400°F.

Roll spoonfuls into small balls and place on a lined oven tray. Press down with a fork and sprinkle with finely chopped walnuts or pinenuts. Alternatively, roll the dough out and use a cookie cutter to stamp out rounds.

Bake for 12–15 minutes until lightly coloured, then remove to a rack to cool.

MAKES 18 X 6 CM (2½″) BISCUITS

125 g (1 cup) self-raising flour, sifted
125 g (4½ oz) unsalted butter, at room temperature
freshly ground black pepper
125 g (4½ oz) Dolce Latte or other similar mild creamy blue cheese
walnuts or pinenuts, finely chopped

parmesan risotto cakes

At the time Philippe Mouchel visited our school in 1995 he was chef at the renowned Paul Bocuse restaurant in Melbourne. These little rice cakes have been adapted from a recipe cooked by Philippe. They can be served as an hors d'oeuvre or as an accompaniment to a meat dish. This no-stir method (see page 194) is fast and easy, although in this instance it is essential to cook the mixture further until quite stiff. If it is too wet the cakes will fall apart. Flavour variations are boundless but try fresh herbs, blue cheese, lemon zest or pesto.

melt the butter in a small, heavy-based saucepan and sauté the shallots gently, without browning, until soft and translucent.

Add the rice and stir to coat in the butter. 'Toast' the rice until warm, then add all the boiling stock. Cover and simmer over a very low heat for 15 minutes until the rice is tender, stirring once halfway through.

Remove from the heat, season and add the cheese. Stir over a gentle heat until the mixture is stiff. Turn out onto a cold tray, spreading out into an even layer, and allow to cool completely.

Using wet hands, form into flat cakes. Dip each cake in flour, then in egg and finally in breadcrumbs and fry gently in olive oil until golden. Serve warm, sprinkled with additional Parmesan. If made ahead, reheat gently to serve.

MAKES APPROXIMATELY 24

25 g ($^3/_4$ oz) butter

30 g (approximately 4) shallots, finely chopped

125 g ($^1/_2$ cup) Ferron rice

250 ml (1 cup) chicken stock, boiling

sea salt and freshly ground pepper

25 g ($^3/_4$ oz) Parmesan cheese, grated

sushi sandwich with pickled vegetables

This is my interpretation of an appetiser served to us the first time I ate at Rock Pool in Sydney – a little taste to whet the appetite and an interesting variation on the familiar rolled sushi.

combine the dressing ingredients and set aside.

Wash the rice several times in cold water and allow to drain for 30 minutes in a sieve. Place the rice in a heavy-based saucepan and add the measured water. Bring quickly to the boil, cover and turn the heat down very low. Steam for 15 minutes without lifting the lid. Remove from the heat and stand, still covered, for 10 minutes.

Turn the rice into a large bowl and pour over the dressing. Mix gently and cool to room temperature.

To assemble, line a shallow square or rectangular tin with plastic wrap. Cover the base of the tin with nori sheets, overlapping slightly at the joins. Firmly press in a 1 cm ($\frac{1}{2}$") layer of rice. Lightly spread with a little wasabi and cover with another layer of nori.

Carefully add another layer of rice the same thickness, finishing with more nori sheets. Cover well and allow to rest in a cool place but do not refrigerate. Carefully remove from the tin to a board and, using a long, wet knife, cut into small squares, approximately 3 cm ($1\frac{1}{4}$") square. Just before serving, top with a small pile of pickled vegetables.

2 cups sushi rice (short grain)
2 cups water
1 packet toasted nori sheets
wasabi paste (optional)

DRESSING FOR RICE
4 tablespoons rice vinegar
3 tablespoons sugar
2 teaspoons salt
2 tablespoons mirin or dry sherry

MAKES ABOUT 36

pickled vegetables

using a mandolin, cut the vegetables into a very fine julienne.

Heat the vinegar and sugar in a saucepan, stirring to dissolve the sugar. Bring to the boil, remove from the heat, cool a little and add all the vegetables except the cucumber.

Pickle for 2 hours, drain and add the cucumber.

1 carrot, peeled
$\frac{1}{2}$ telegraph cucumber, peeled and seeded
1 small daikon radish, peeled
2 spring onions
pickled ginger
500 ml (2 cups) rice vinegar
$1\frac{1}{2}$ cups caster sugar

thai fish cakes with chilli and cucumber salad

A food processor makes light work of turning the fish into a smooth paste for these little cakes. The good thing is that they can be made ahead and eaten cold or reheated very gently and eaten warm. The chilli and cucumber salad is delicious mounded on top or simply have some sweet chilli sauce in a little bowl for dipping.

remove any trace of skin or bone from the fish fillets and cut into small pieces. Place in a food processor and process until smooth. Add the red curry paste, fish sauce, cornflour, egg and ginger. Process again until a smooth paste is formed.

Place the mixture in a bowl and stir in the chilli, spring onion and coriander.

Heat 1 cm (½") of oil in a frying pan over a medium heat. With oiled hands, form 1 tablespoon portions of the mixture into flat round cakes. Fry a few at a time until a deep golden brown underneath. Turn the cakes over carefully and fry the other side. Remove with a slotted spoon and drain on paper towels.

SERVES ?

300 g (10½ oz) firm white fish fillets
2 teaspoons red curry paste
1 tablespoon fish sauce
1 tablespoon cornflour
1 egg, beaten
1 teaspoon fresh ginger, grated
1 teaspoon finely chopped fresh red chilli
2 spring onions, finely chopped
2 tablespoons fresh coriander leaves, chopped
vegetable oil for frying

chilli and cucumber salad

dissolve the sugar in the fish sauce and lime juice and dilute with a little water if it appears too strong. Add the vegetables and just before serving drain and place a small pile on the top of each cake.

MAKES 1 CUP

2 tablespoons sugar
2 tablespoons fish sauce
2 tablespoons lime juice
water
½ cup cucumber, seeded and very finely sliced
2 teaspoons shallot, very finely sliced
1 fresh red chilli, sliced

sweetcorn fritters

When Australian cook Meera Freeman visited our school, her enthusiasm for the cuisines of Asia, especially Vietnam, was infectious. I have always felt privileged that I have the opportunity to spend time with so many of our guest chefs. Together we visit our markets, eat out and cook together. Meera taught me a great deal about Asian ingredients and cooking methods. This is one of the simplest dishes she cooked. Serve the fritters, called 'tord man kaopot', with the cucumber and chilli salad on page 130, or garnish with coriander leaves and serve a bowl of sweet chilli sauce for dipping.

cut the corn from the cobs with a sharp knife. This should yield about 100 grams (4 oz) from each cob.

Place in the bowl of a food processor together with the rice and plain flours, curry powder and soy sauce and process until the ingredients are well blended but not too finely chopped. The texture is better if the corn niblets are still discernible.

Heat the oil in a frying pan and slip spoonfuls of the corn mixture into the pan, a few at a time, cooking over a moderate heat until the patties are golden on one side. Turn and fry on the other side.

Drain well on paper towels and serve warm at room temperature, garnished with coriander leaves.

MAKES APPROXIMATELY 24

3 fresh corn cobs
2 tablespoons rice flour
3 tablespoons plain flour
1 teaspoon curry powder
2 tablespoons light soy sauce
vegetable oil for frying
1 tablespoon coriander leaves

OTHER SMALL BITES IN THIS BOOK:

Peking Duck Pancakes with Plum Sauce
Chinese Steamed Dumplings
Italian Bread Skewers with Pancetta and Feta
Tunisian Eggplant Confit
Sicilian Marinated Olives
Gorgonzola Risotto Balls
Green Olive 'Fritters'

Rock Oysters with Ginger Soy Sambal
Oysters with Lime and Sesame
Tomato Tarts
Asparagus with Anchovy Cream
Rock Oysters with Garlic and Herbs
Baked Feta with Lemon
Smoked Fish and Kumara Cakes

an asian feast

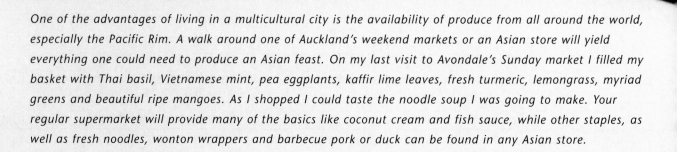

One of the advantages of living in a multicultural city is the availability of produce from all around the world, especially the Pacific Rim. A walk around one of Auckland's weekend markets or an Asian store will yield everything one could need to produce an Asian feast. On my last visit to Avondale's Sunday market I filled my basket with Thai basil, Vietnamese mint, pea eggplants, kaffir lime leaves, fresh turmeric, lemongrass, myriad greens and beautiful ripe mangoes. As I shopped I could taste the noodle soup I was going to make. Your regular supermarket will provide many of the basics like coconut cream and fish sauce, while other staples, as well as fresh noodles, wonton wrappers and barbecue pork or duck can be found in any Asian store.

chinese steamed dumplings

Clare Ferguson, cook and food stylist extraordinaire, makes an annual pilgrimage back to her homeland and we love to have her cook at Epicurean. Her classes are tremendous fun, the food inspired and always very delicious. She treats us to tales of her travels and her time spent at her Greek island hideaway. This recipe for shao mai is adapted from one she taught us, as are the dipping suggestions at the end. You could, of course, replace the pork, prawn, or both with chicken.

mix the prawn meat and pork mince, white pepper and wine in a bowl. Cover and set aside while the other ingredients are prepared.

In a second bowl, whisk the egg white to a froth, then beat in the sesame oil, ginger, salt, garlic and parsley.

Slowly beat into the meat mixture, adding the spring onion and water chestnuts as well, until evenly combined, but not over-mixed.

Using a large biscuit cutter, cut a round as large as possible from each square wonton wrapper. Put 1 tablespoon of filling on each wonton wrapper and, using a small spatula, smooth the mixture almost to the edges.

Put the filled wonton in the palm of one hand and cup your fingers around it, pushing the mixture down with the spatula – you will achieve an open, pleated purse shape. Drop it gently onto a floured clean surface to flatten the bottom and settle the filling.

Arrange the dumplings, without letting them touch each other, on the base of a well oiled bamboo steamer. Heat a wok or pan of boiling water on top of the stove, set the steamer on top and steam the dumplings, covered, for about 7–10 minutes, refilling the base with boiling water as necessary. Serve hot, topped with chives or coriander, with a variety of dipping sauces.

250 g (9 oz) prawn meat, finely chopped

250 g (9 oz) pork mince

1 teaspoon freshly ground white pepper

2 tablespoons shao-hsing rice wine

1 egg white

2 teaspoons sesame oil

2 teaspoons grated fresh ginger

2 teaspoons sea salt flakes

2 teaspoons crushed garlic

2 tablespoons finely chopped parsley

4 spring onions, green and white, finely chopped

4 water chestnuts, canned or fresh and peeled, finely diced

30–45 square wonton wrappers

sprigs of Chinese chives, chives or coriander

MAKES APPROXIMATELY 36

Sauces and 'wet' dipping mixtures can be assembled from ready-made condiments with ease. Try – sesame oil and soy sauce, mixed; chilli oil with finely sliced spring onion tops; fresh ginger shreds with hoisin sauce; sweet chilli sauce; yellow bean sauce and fresh citrus juice, mixed; balsamic vinaigrette.

'Dry' dipping mixtures: roasted peppercorns and sea salt, ground; Szechwan peppercorns, toasted and ground with sugar and powdered ginger; chopped green herbs and chopped garlic, mixed; toasted sesame seeds; black onion seeds; chopped dry-roasted peanuts.

peking duck pancakes with plum sauce

Roast duck, purchased from your local Asian barbecue shop, is a quick and easy ingredient. Once all the meat has been removed, the bones can be made into a delicious broth to serve as noodle soup with a few greens and any leftover pieces of duck meat. Place the bones in a large pot and cover with water. Add lemongrass, garlic, ginger and star anise and simmer gently for an hour. Strain and it's ready to use.

remove the duck meat from the bone and slice.

To make the pancakes, sift the flour and salt into a bowl. Combine the eggs, milk and water, add to the dry ingredients and beat until smooth. Cover lightly and let stand for 30–60 minutes.

To cook: lightly oil a 15–18 cm/6–7" skillet (preferably non-stick) and place over a low heat. Stir the batter and, off the heat, pour a small amount (about 2 tablespoons) into the skillet. Rotate the pan to cover the bottom with batter, and pour out any excess. Cook until set but not browned. Turn and cook the other side. Remove the pancake and cool on a clean towel. Continue until all the batter is used, brushing the skillet with oil as necessary.

Brush a little plum sauce over the inside of a pancake. Wrap a few slices of duck meat and cucumber inside each and fold over. Serve at room temperature.

MAKES 32 PANCAKES

1 Peking roast duck

PANCAKES
1$\frac{1}{2}$ cups plain flour
$\frac{1}{4}$ teaspoon salt
2 eggs, beaten
1$\frac{1}{2}$ cups (375 ml) milk
1 cup (250 ml) water
oil for frying

plum sauce
very thin slices of cucumber

spicy coconut soup with sliced chicken and cellophane noodles

All the ingredients in this soup can be readily found in most supermarkets these days, except perhaps the kaffir lime leaves. These are available fresh at Asian green grocers, or you could plant your own aromatic tree. This style of dish is a favourite, not just for it's simplicity but for it's delicious flavours and the comfort factor that all noodle soups provide.

preheat the oven to 200°C/400°F.

Mix together the garlic, sugar and soy sauce and coat the chicken well. Bake until cooked through. Remove from the oven and allow to rest, loosely covered.

Soak the cellophane noodles in boiling water to soften. Drain, toss in a little oil and set aside.

Place the chicken stock, coriander, ginger, lime leaves, chillies, lemongrass and shallots in a saucepan. Bring to the boil and simmer for 10 minutes.

Add the mushrooms and coconut cream and simmer for 3 minutes. Discard the lemongrass.

Add the fish sauce, lime juice and soaked noodles and bring to the boil but do not cover.

Divide the soup and noodles between 4 plates. Slice the chicken and place on top. Garnish with coriander leaves.

SERVES 4

CHICKEN

2 cloves garlic, crushed to a paste
1 tablespoon sugar
4 teaspoons soy sauce
4 single chicken breasts

200 g (7 oz) cellophane noodles
vegetable oil

SOUP

600 ml (21 fl oz) homemade chicken stock
3 tablespoons finely chopped coriander stalks
2 tablespoons finely chopped fresh ginger
4 kaffir lime leaves, fresh or dried
3 small dried red chillies, chopped
1 large bulb lemongrass, crushed
3 shallots, thinly sliced
1 cup thinly sliced button mushrooms
400 ml (14 fl oz) coconut cream
3 tablespoons fish sauce
4 tablespoons lime juice
coriander leaves to garnish

green papaya salad

This is one of those dishes that can only be made if you can find the vital ingredient, in this case green papaya. Often the stores, unless it is an Asian one, will keep unripe papayas out back until they have ripened, so it's best to ask. Use a regular cheese grater to shred the papaya and serve the salad as a first course or as part of a feast.

in a large bowl, combine the lime juice, fish sauce and palm sugar and stir to dissolve the sugar. Stir in the garlic and chilli and mix well.

Add the papaya, mint, coriander and spring onion to the dressing. Using your hands, gently squeeze the mixture to release the flavours and soften the vegetables. Add the shrimp powder, peanuts and sesame seeds and toss well.

To serve, mound the salad on a platter and garnish with mint sprigs.

SERVES 4

DRESSING

$\frac{1}{4}$ cup (4 tablespoons) fresh lime juice

3 tablespoons fish sauce

2 teaspoons palm sugar

1 tablespoon crushed garlic

2 tablespoons finely chopped red or green chilli

3 cups peeled, seeded and shredded green (unripe) papaya

$\frac{1}{4}$ cup coarsely chopped fresh mint

$\frac{1}{4}$ cup coarsely chopped fresh coriander

3 tablespoons finely chopped spring onion

1 tablespoon dried shrimp powder

2 tablespoons roughly chopped unsalted dry-roasted peanuts

2 tablespoons sesame seeds, lightly toasted

fresh mint to garnish

spring vegetable curry

The spices in this dish are very special. Its roots are Sri Lankan and everyone at Epicurean, including our Sri Lankan kitchen assistant Malka, found this curry delicious. Recipe testing time is very popular and we all eat very well indeed. If you grind spices frequently, a good investment is a electric coffee grinder, which does the job very quickly and efficiently. The flavours of freshly toasted and ground spices cannot be compared with a store-bought equivalent.

toast the whole spices – cumin, fennel, coriander, fenugreek and mustard seed separately, over a low heat in a small skillet, until fragrant. Grind and combine with the remaining ground spices.

Combine the tomatoes, water, 1 teaspoon of salt, 2 tablespoons of the ginger and 1 tablespoon of the spice mix in a medium saucepan. Bring to the boil and simmer, uncovered, for 15–20 minutes.

Meanwhile, blanch the different peas in boiling, salted water. Refresh under cold water and set aside.

Heat the peanut oil in a large skillet. Add the onion with a little salt and sauté gently until soft. Add the garlic, carrots and potatoes and cook for 10 minutes. Add the cauliflower, courgette and the remaining ginger and spice mix. Sauté for a further 5 minutes and add the tomato mixture and coconut cream. Simmer, uncovered, for 30 minutes. Just before serving, add the peas. Season with salt and cayenne to taste.

SERVES 4–6 WITH RICE

SPICE MIX
1 teaspoon each cumin seed, fennel seed
2 teaspoons coriander seed
$\frac{1}{2}$ teaspoon each fenugreek, black mustard seed, ground cinnamon
$\frac{1}{4}$ teaspoon each ground cardamom, ground cloves, cayenne pepper

CURRY
2 cups tinned tomatoes with juice, chopped
1$\frac{1}{2}$ cups (375 ml) cold water
sea salt
3 tablespoons grated fresh ginger
100 g (4 oz) sugar snap peas or snow peas
100 g (4 oz) English peas
1 tablespoon peanut oil
1 onion, chopped
4 cloves garlic, finely chopped
2 medium carrots, cut in half lengthways, sliced on the diagonal
500 g (1 lb) new potatoes, quartered
$\frac{1}{2}$ small cauliflower cut into florets
1 courgette, cut the same as the carrot
1$\frac{1}{2}$ cups (375 ml) coconut cream
cayenne pepper

139

green beans with coconut

We all have our favourite recipes, gathered over the years from family, friends and books. This is one of Jacqueline's which she shared with us in 'Gourmet on the Run' this year.

trim the beans and set aside.

Heat the oil in a heavy-based frying pan over a medium heat. Add the shallot and garlic and fry for a few minutes.

Add the mustard and cumin seeds and when the mustard seeds begin to pop add the curry leaves, chilli and turmeric.

Stir for a few minutes then add the coconut and salt. Stir for a few minutes more then add the beans and water.

Bring to the boil and simmer until the beans are tender and the water has evaporated. Season if needed with extra salt.

SERVES 6

500 g (1 lb) round green beans
2 tablespoons vegetable oil
1 large shallot, chopped
2 cloves garlic, chopped
1 tablespoon mustard seeds
2 teaspoons cumin seeds
10 fresh curry leaves
1–2 chillies, sliced
$\frac{1}{2}$ teaspoon turmeric
$\frac{3}{4}$ cup coconut threads
1 teaspoon salt
1 cup (250 ml) hot water

twice cooked quail

When Nicholas Huffman cooked this dish at the Epicurean, his restaurant had just won the prestigious Corbans Wine and Food Challenge. Nicholas is now at the helm of the Huka Lodge kitchens, and very much at the forefront of fine New Zealand cuisine. This is an incredibly simple dish. The first stage can be done well ahead, with stage two taking a matter of minutes.

combine the first 7 ingredients in a saucepan and bring to the boil. Add the quail and simmer for 5 minutes. Take off the heat and stand for 10 minutes. Remove the quail and place on a cake rack to drain. Strain the poaching liquid, discarding the solids. Reserve.

Heat the peanut oil in a wok or large pan and shallow fry the quail until crisp and brown. Keep warm.

Pour off excess oil leaving just a tablespoon in the pan. Stirfry the vegetables and glaze with ½ cup of the reserved poaching liquor.

Place the vegetables on each plate or one large platter and put the quail on top.

SERVES 4

500 ml (2 cups) Kikkoman soy sauce
300 ml (10½ fl oz) sake
300 ml (10½ fl oz) mirin
6 star anise
50 g (1¾ oz) fresh ginger
2 cloves garlic
1 red chilli

4 quail, halved and back bone removed.

500 ml (2 cups) peanut oil
1 Chinese cabbage, sliced and blanched briefly
1 bunch asparagus, trimmed and blanched
12 shiitake mushrooms, cleaned, trimmed and sliced

pork with grilled bok choy, steamed rice and ponzu sauce

Ray McVinnie cooked this dish in a barbecue class way back in 1995. I still prepare it and have a jar of ponzu sauce in the fridge at all times.

All the ingredients for this can be found at an Asian store. Cook the pork until it is really, really crispy and brown all over. Sliced thinly, a little goes a long way.

combine the sauce ingredients and allow to stand for 24 hours. Strain through muslin into a clean jar and store for up to 1 year in the refrigerator – it gets better and better.

mix the marinade ingredients together and pour over the pork. Marinate overnight or for a minimum of 2 hours.

Blanch the bok choy in boiling water for 2–3 minutes, refresh in cold water, drain well and lightly toss in vegetable oil.

Cook the pork on a lightly oiled grill over a gentle heat until the skin is crisp and the pork is well cooked. Remove from the heat and slice thinly.

At the same time grill the bok choy until hot and browned.

Serve with the rice in individual bowls or all together on a large platter with the ponzu in a small bowl as a dipping sauce.

SERVES 4–6

PONZU SAUCE
1 cup lemon juice
$\frac{1}{3}$ cup rice vinegar
1 cup dark soy sauce
2 tablespoons tamari sauce
3 tablespoons mirin
10 g (1$\frac{1}{2}$ cups) bonito flakes (dried fish)
5 cm (2") square piece of konbu (giant kelp)

MARINADE
4 tablespoons fish sauce
4 tablespoons soy sauce
1 tablespoon ginger, finely sliced
2 cloves garlic, finely chopped
1 tablespoon sugar

600 g (1 lb 5 oz) pork belly or loin sliced 2–3 cm ($\frac{3}{4}$"–1$\frac{1}{4}$") thick, boned, skin on
6 baby bok choy, quartered lengthwise
vegetable oil
2 cups hot steamed long grain rice

lime, ginger and mango brûlée tart

It would be very unusual to be served a dessert such as this in Asia. However, we love the fresh mango and lime flavours that chef Mark Nicholson created for the filling and think it makes a fitting end to an Asian feast.

in a large bowl, dissolve the sugar in the lime juice, mixing well. Add the eggs and combine. Add the cream and stir well.

Pass the mixture though a sieve and leave to stand in the fridge for 2 hours. Skim off any froth that rises to the surface.

Preheat the oven to 200°C/400°F.

Meanwhile, roll out the sweet pastry and line a 32 cm x 2.5 cm (12" x 1") flan tin with a removable base. Rest in the fridge for 20 minutes before baking blind (see page 194).

Reduce the oven temperature to 130°C/260°F.

Arrange the mango slices in the base of the pastry case. Place the tart tin on a baking tray.

Add the grated ginger and lime zest to the egg mixture and pour carefully over the mangoes until the tart is nearly full. Transfer the tart, on the tray, to the oven and continue filling to the top.

Bake for about 45 minutes or until the filling is just set. Allow to cool.

SERVES 8–10

400 g (14 oz) caster sugar
1 cup (250 ml) lime juice – about 9 limes
9 eggs
1 cup (250 ml) cream
1 quantity sweet short pastry (pate sucrée) (see page 195)
1 tin mango pieces, drained and sliced
1 small piece fresh ginger, peeled and grated
zest of 4 limes

casual winter dining

There is always a time of year that signals the beginning of winter – it's when you suddenly feel the desire for a big bowl of soup. This is comfort food that gives us a sense of warmth and security. It is also simple food – a hearty casserole with a chunk of bread to sop up the gravy, a big plate of steaming risotto or a luscious sticky pudding like grandma used to make. It often brings back memories, too. For me, as a child, it is Sunday night suppers in front of the fire or, with luck, the television. Today, it is more likely to mean a relaxed evening with pressures forgotten, if only temporarily.

baked feta with lemon

This combination, also from Ray McVinnie, is a magic one, but it's important to use a firm feta, one that has small pockets filled with whey, rather than a smooth, creamy one. If you find the feta salty, simply soak it in water for a little while and then drain. This is good served on its own as described below or as part of an antipasti plate. I also enjoy this baked feta tossed through a plate of hot, cooked orzo (see page 35).

preheat the oven to 200°C/400°F.

Break the feta into chunks and put onto a shallow baking tray.

Combine the other ingredients and spoon over the feta. Bake until the feta has browned on the edges.

Pile on a plate, drizzle with more olive oil, garnish with lemon wedges and serve with fresh crusty bread.

500 g (1 lb) firm cow's feta

4 tablespoons extra virgin olive oil

1 tablespoon finely diced preserved lemon (see page 195)

1 clove garlic, finely chopped

freshly ground pepper

lemon wedges

rock oyster with garlic and herbs

Although I still maintain that the best way to eat oysters is chilled, sometimes they can be very good served just warmed through. This dish from Ray McVinnie could be prepared using Bluff oysters, serving them on Chinese spoons instead of in the shell.

detach the oysters from their shells, reserving any liquor and the shells. Arrange the shells on a platter.

Bring the lime juice, fish sauce and sugar to the boil in a small saucepan. Taste and season with salt and pepper, if needed.

Heat a little oil in a skillet and gently fry the garlic, chilli, ginger and lemongrass until aromatic.

Stir in the mint and add the oysters. Stirfry gently until the oysters colour and are just warmed through.

Put the oysters back in their shells along with some of the herbs. Spoon over the hot sauce and serve garnished with fresh mint and lemon.

SERVES 6 AS A FIRST COURSE

3 dozen rock oysters, in the shell
$\frac{1}{2}$ cup (125 ml) lime juice
$\frac{1}{2}$ cup (125 ml) fish sauce
3 tablespoons sugar
sea salt and freshly ground pepper
vegetable oil
4 cloves garlic, finely chopped
1 small fresh chilli, seeded and finely chopped
2 tablespoon ginger, finely chopped
2 tablespoons lemongrass, bulb only, finely chopped
2 tablespoons fresh mint, finely chopped
mint leaves and lemons

smoked fish and kumara hash cakes
with beetroot relish and sour cream

Laurie Black is a young chef, who, when she is not catering, is an up and coming food stylist. Our classes on food for cocktail parties are always considered a challenge by the chefs we invite to take them. Laurie rose to the challenge with her class entitled 'Reality Bites'. She included many easy ideas, including the 'oysters, two ways' on page 92 and these little smoked fish cakes. Make these cakes bigger and serve them as a first course or for brunch.

place the fish, bayleaf and peppercorns in a saucepan and cover with milk. Bring to the boil, reduce the heat and simmer for 10 minutes. Drain, discarding the bayleaf and peppercorns.

Place the garlic and kumara in a large pot of salted water, bring to the boil and simmer until tender. Drain.

Squeeze the garlic from its skin and mash with the kumara.

Beat in half the egg and the remaining ingredients. Add the rest of the egg if the mixture is very stiff. Chill until firm.

Form into small cakes, about 3 cm (1¼") thick. Dust lightly with flour and gently pan fry in olive oil until browned. Remove from the pan and place on baking paper on a tray.

Refrigerate until required.

meanwhile, preheat the oven to 180°C/350°F.

Place the whole beetroot in a roasting pan and bake until just tender. Cool and peel. Grate the beetroot and place in a saucepan with the remaining ingredients. Simmer until a little syrupy. Cool. Refrigerated, it will keep for up to 6 weeks.

To serve, transfer the fish cakes to a baking sheet and bake for 10 minutes at 175°C/350°F. Place on a serving tray and top with a little sour cream and beetroot relish.

MAKES ABOUT 40 CAKES WITH 1½ CUPS RELISH

170 g (6 oz) boned and smoked white fish, e.g. ruby, gem, tarakihi
1 bayleaf
4 whole black peppercorns
milk for poaching
1 whole head garlic, broken into cloves
2 large yellow kumara (about 850 g/ 1¾ lb), peeled and chopped into small dice
1 egg, beaten
2 tablespoons chopped dill
¼ cup flour, sifted
1 tablespoon lemon juice
salt and pepper
extra flour
olive oil for frying

BEETROOT RELISH
2 medium beetroot
¾ cup brown sugar
1 clove garlic, sliced
2 teaspoons coriander seeds, toasted and coarsely ground
black pepper
julienned zest and juice of 2 oranges
¼ cup wine vinegar

sour cream

mussel, riesling and curry broth

Melbourne is known as a culinary mecca. It's also a city where young British chefs seem to congregate. Jeremy Strode is one of the 'young Brits' who has made a name for himself, first at the Adelphi and now at his own establishment, Pomme. On his visit to us a few years ago, he prepared this aromatic soup using one of our nation's best foods, greenlip mussels.

heat the oil in a heavy bottomed pan with deep sides. Add half the onion plus the garlic, celery, thyme, parsley and peppercorns. Stir, add the mussels and the Riesling and cover with a lid.

Cook over a high heat until the mussels open. Drain, reserving the mussel liquor, and cover with a damp cloth.

In another pan, melt 2 tablespoons of the butter, add the remaining onion and cook until soft, but not brown. Add the curry powder and cook over a low heat for 10 minutes.

Add the reserved mussel liquor and bring to the boil. Add the cream, return to the boil and then reduce the heat to simmer for 5 minutes. Season with white pepper.

Meanwhile, remove the mussels from their shells. Divide them between warm soup plates. Sprinkle with tomato and chives.

Using a handheld blender, gradually add the remaining butter to the curry broth, achieving a froth. Pour over the mussels gently and serve.

SERVES 4 AS A MAIN COURSE OR 6 AS A FIRST COURSE

2 tablespoons vegetable oil

2 onions, chopped

4 cloves garlic, finely sliced

1 celery stick, chopped

4 sprigs fresh thyme

6 parsley stalks

1 teaspoon white peppercorns

40 small to medium mussels, scrubbed and beards removed

1 cup (250 ml) Riesling

100 g (4 oz) unsalted butter, chilled and diced

2 teaspoons curry powder

200 ml (7 fl oz) cream

freshly ground white pepper

1 tomato, blanched, peeled, seeded and diced

1 tablespoon finely chopped chives

north beach cioppino

One of my most favourite restaurants in San Francisco is Rose Pistola in the North Beach area where immigrant Italians from Liguria made their new home.

I love the antipasti set out on long oval platters, at one end of the long counter, which are served individually on small plates. And I love the wood-fired ovens, extending down one side of the room, which produce everything from pizza to this wonderful seafood soup made with red wine. For this reason I always sit at the counter so I can watch the chefs at work and chat to them about the different dishes. This is my version of their cioppino.

heat the oil in a large saucepan over a medium high heat. Add the onion, garlic and capsicum and cook, stirring frequently, for 5 minutes or until the vegetables begin to soften. Add the drained tomatoes, breaking them up with a spoon, and cook, stirring frequently, for 5 minutes.

Stir in the tomato paste, herbs, wine, salt and black pepper and cook over a medium heat for 20 minutes.

Add the fish and shellfish and cook covered for 5 minutes or until the shellfish have opened and the prawns have turned pink and opaque.

Serve in deep bowls with crusty bread.

SERVES 4–6

2 tablespoons olive oil

1 large onion, finely sliced

3 cloves garlic, chopped

**1 large green capsicum, seeded and
    sliced**

**2$\frac{1}{2}$ cups (2 x 400 g [14 oz] tins) tinned
    tomatoes, coarsely chopped and
    drained**

2 tablespoons tomato paste

**$\frac{1}{4}$ teaspoon each dried basil, dried
    oregano, dried thyme**

**$\frac{1}{4}$ teaspoon dried chilli flakes
    (optional)**

$\frac{1}{4}$ cup Italian parsley leaves, chopped

2 cups (500 ml) dry red wine

sea salt and freshly ground pepper

500 g (1 lb) firm fish, cut into chunks

**selection of mussels, prawns, cockles
    or tuatua**

veal meatballs with fresh marjoram and tomatoes

I think most cooks have their own favourite meatball recipe. This is mine and it's one I cook often. Sometimes I serve it with some crusty bread and a salad to follow, but other times I team it with creamy polenta (page 195) or penne pasta. It's rustic, hearty fare – perfect for a winter weekend lunch.

soak the bread in the milk. Squeeze out the excess moisture and combine in a large bowl with the veal, garlic, eggs, zest, Parmesan and half the marjoram. Season well and roll the mixture into 2.5 cm (1") balls.

Toss the meatballs in flour and shake off the excess.

Heat the olive oil in a large frying pan. Add the meatballs and brown them (in batches if necessary) over a medium heat.

Drain off all but 2 tablespoons of the oil. Add the tomatoes, the remaining marjoram and salt to taste. Simmer for 10 minutes or until the sauce thickens.

Serve with creamy polenta, pasta or plenty of good bread.

SERVES 4

1 thick slice bread (about 40 g/1$\frac{1}{2}$ oz), crust removed
$\frac{1}{3}$ cup milk
500 g (1 lb) veal mince
2 cloves garlic, crushed
2 eggs, lightly beaten
zest of $\frac{1}{2}$ lemon
$\frac{1}{4}$ cup grated Parmesan cheese
2 tablespoons fresh marjoram, chopped
sea salt and freshly ground pepper
plain flour
6 tablespoons extra virgin olive oil
400 g (14 oz) tin Italian tomatoes, seeded and chopped, with juice

creamy polenta with winter sauce

Sauces like this one or the sausage and fennel one on page 157 can be made ahead and reheated to serve. The flavours will improve if left to develop for a day or two in the fridge.

place the chicken stock, cream and garlic into a large pot and heat until boiling. Add the grated Parmesan. Slowly pour in the polenta and semolina, whisking to combine. Cook over a low temperature for 20 minutes. Polenta is cooked when it comes away from the sides of the pan. Season well with salt and pepper.

Melt 1 tablespoon of the butter in a large sauté pan. Add the mushrooms and sauté over a high heat until tender. Remove to a bowl, reserving any liquid in the pan as well.

In the same pan, melt the other 2 tablespoons of butter and add the onion, pancetta or bacon and the rosemary. Cook gently until the onion is tender and the pancetta has rendered its fat. Add the sausage, increase the heat and cook, browning slightly and breaking up the meat with a wooden spoon.

After 5 minutes, add the wine and allow to evaporate. Add the tomatoes and their juice and season with salt and pepper. Continue to cook gently and after 10 minutes add the mushrooms and reserved juices. Cook a further 10 minutes until the sauce is thick. Adjust the seasoning.

Ladle the polenta into shallow soup bowls and top with the sauce. Sprinkle generously with Parmesan and parsley.

SERVES 6

POLENTA

2 litres (3$\frac{1}{2}$ pints) chicken stock

1 cup (250 ml) cream

2 teaspoons crushed garlic

$\frac{1}{2}$ cup Parmesan cheese, freshly grated

$\frac{3}{4}$ cup instant polenta

1 cup semolina

salt and freshly ground black pepper

SAUCE

3 tablespoons butter

100 g (4 oz) medium sized brown button mushrooms, sliced

1 medium onion, diced finely

4 slices pancetta or bacon, chopped

2 sprigs fresh rosemary leaves, chopped

3 sweet Italian sausages, casings removed

$\frac{1}{4}$ cup dry white wine

2 x 400 g (14 oz) tins Italian tomatoes, with juice, crushed

salt and freshly ground pepper

freshly grated Parmesan cheese and chopped Italian parsley to serve

penne with sausage and fennel

Penne pasta is that thick, diagonally cut, tube pasta that is designed to be filled with a chunky sauce. A good rule to remember is that thin pasta, such as linguine or fettuccine, needs a thin sauce and thick hollow pasta needs something thick that will fill it up. Good quality pasta also has a rough surface to which the sauce will adhere, all of which goes into making the dish truly memorable.

heat the olive oil in a medium frying pan. Add the onion and sauté gently until it begins to soften. Add the fennel and cook with the onion until both are soft. Increase the heat and add the garlic and sausage. Brown the sausage and then add the herbs, stock and wine. Season and reduce the heat to a simmer. Cook the sauce until it thickens. Add the cream and cook 5 minutes longer.

When the sauce is ready, cook the pasta in abundant boiling, salted water.

Drain and toss with the sauce. Transfer to a large serving bowl and garnish with grated Parmesan and parsley.

SERVES 4–6

$^1/_4$ **cup extra virgin olive oil**
$^1/_2$ **medium onion, chopped**
2 fennel bulbs, thinly sliced
2 cloves garlic, crushed
300 g (10$^1/_2$ oz) Italian sausage, casings removed
small handful of basil and oregano leaves, shredded
$^1/_2$ **cup (125 ml) chicken stock**
$^1/_2$ **cup (125 ml) red wine**
sea salt and freshly ground pepper
$^1/_2$ **cup (125 ml) cream (optional)**
450 g (1 lb) good quality penne pasta
grated Parmesan and chopped Italian parsley to garnish

roasted pumpkin and pancetta risotto

The beauty of risotto is that it can be flavoured with any ingredients you have on hand. In Everyday Epicurean there are asparagus, shellfish and porcini mushroom risottos, but basically the ideas are boundless. This one, sweet with roasted pumpkin, is a favourite to which I sometimes add some finely shredded spinach at the end.

preheat the oven to 200°C/400°F. Place the pumpkin in a roasting pan and drizzle with a little olive oil, turning to coat. Roast for 20–30 minutes or until tender. Add the pancetta towards the end, and cook, but do not allow to become crisp.

Heat a little oil in a large pot and sauté the garlic and onion slowly.

Add the rice and heat for a few minutes. Add the boiling stock all at once. Bring to the boil, add salt, cover and reduce to a simmer. Cook for 15 minutes, stirring about halfway through.

Add the pancetta, pumpkin and Parmigiano and fold through. Season, rest for a few minutes and serve.

SERVES 6–8

450 g (1 lb) pumpkin, peeled, seeded and cubed

extra virgin olive oil

40 g (1$\frac{1}{2}$ oz) pancetta or bacon, chopped

2–4 cloves garlic, crushed (optional)

1 red onion or 4 shallots, chopped

2 cups Ferron risotto rice – Vialone Nano

4 cups (1 litre) chicken stock, boiling

40 g (1$\frac{1}{2}$ oz) Parmigiano Reggiano, grated

sea salt and freshly ground pepper

lemon and sage risotto with roast cornfed chicken

1999 was the year of risotto in New Zealand. It started with a visit by Gabriele Ferron in March when he extolled the virtues of both his rice and his no-stir cooking method for risotto. Although I had known about his method for some time, I had remained a sceptic until I learned about it firsthand. Since then I have experimented and discovered that the method works beautifully, as long as you use the Ferron rice. The reasons are legitimate. Ferron rice is milled by hand and therefore retains most of the starch that is required to make a good risotto. Other commercially milled rices have had most of the starch removed and therefore need constant stirring to release what starch is left. Confused? Read about the two methods on page 194.

preheat the oven to 200°C/400°F.

Stuff the chicken with half a lemon, the sage and a good grind of pepper. Tuck the wings underneath and tie the parson's nose and legs together. Smear the chicken with a little butter and place, breast down, in a roasting pan. Add the neck and the water. Roast for 30 minutes, then turn breast up. Baste and return to the oven for approximately 45 minutes until the legs wobble freely and the juices run clear. Rest 10 minutes before carving.

To make the risotto, heat the olive oil in a large, heavy-based pan and gently soften the onion. Add the lemon zest, sage and rice and toss to coat in the oil. 'Toast' the rice until warm and add the chicken stock all at once. Bring to the boil, add a little salt, cover and simmer for 15 minutes, stirring once halfway through.

Remove from the heat and stir through the Parmigiano. Season with extra salt if needed and freshly ground pepper.

Serve in shallow bowls topped with slices of roast chicken and sprinkled with sage which has been dotted with butter and crisped in a hot oven.

SERVES 4

CHICKEN

1.5 kg free-range cornfed chicken
1 lemon
few sprigs of sage
freshly ground pepper
butter
½ cup water

RISOTTO

2–3 tablespoons extra virgin olive oil
1 onion, finely chopped
zest of 1 lemon
2 tablespoons fresh sage, chopped
250 g (9 oz) Vialone Nano rice
2 cups (500 ml) chicken stock, boiling
sea salt and freshly ground pepper
Parmigiano Reggiano

sage leaves and butter

prune and armagnac flan

Patricia Wells continues to be a source of inspiration to me with her books Bistro Cooking *and* Trattoria. *In France a flan has no pastry, making it easy to prepare in comparison to a tart with its pastry case. This one, adapted from* Bistro Cooking *is definitely best served the day it is made. After that it may become rather heavy.*

place the prunes in a bowl and toss with the Armagnac, cover with plastic wrap and set aside to marinate. (This can be done anywhere from 2 days to 2 hours prior to use.)

Preheat the oven to 190°C/375°F. Lightly butter and flour a 27 cm (11") straight sided ceramic baking dish.

Toss 1 tablespoon of sugar with the marinated prunes. Arrange them on the bottom of the prepared baking dish, forming a single tight layer that completely covers the bottom of the dish.

Beat the eggs with 3 tablespoons of the sugar in a large bowl until well blended. Add the flour and mix well. Whisk in the milk and pour the batter over the prunes. Bake until bubbly and brown – about 45 minutes.

Set on a rack. Sprinkle on the remaining 1 tablespoon sugar. Allow to cool. Serve at room temperature with pouring cream.

SERVES 8

500 g (1 lb) prunes, pitted
3 tablespoons Armagnac or brandy
5 tablespoons sugar
3 large eggs
3 tablespoons plus 1 teaspoon plain flour
2 cups (500 ml) milk

chocolate bread pudding

Some years ago, bread and butter puddings made a comeback to our tables, not as the thin, milky versions remembered from our childhoods, but enriched with sweet breads like croissant or brioche and with cream, eggs and spices. This one is further enriched with melted chocolate. Make a large one for informal gatherings or individual puddings to end an elegant dinner. For small puddings you will need to cut the brioche cubes smaller.

preheat the oven to 180°C/350°F and lightly butter a 30 x 22 cm (12 x 9") baking dish or 10–12 ramekins.

Place the brioche cubes in a large mixing bowl.

Heat the cream until hot but not boiling. Remove from the heat, add the chocolate and stir until melted. Place the mixture in a food processor and add the sugar, egg yolks, butter, vanilla and cinnamon and process until smooth.

Pour the mixture over the bread cubes and toss to coat.

Beat the egg whites and salt until they hold stiff peaks. Fold gently into the chocolate mixture until thoroughly incorporated.

Spoon the mixture into the prepared baking dish or ramekins and place in a roasting pan, then transfer the pan to the shelf of the oven. Fill the roasting pan with boiling water to come halfway up the side of the baking dish.

Bake for 50–60 minutes for a large one or about 30 minutes for small ones.

Serve warm with whipped cream.

SERVES 8–10

1 large brioche, cut into large cubes
1 cup (250 ml) cream
250 g (9 oz) good quality dark chocolate, grated
$\frac{1}{2}$ cup sugar
5 large eggs, separated
85 g (3 oz) unsalted butter at room temperature
2 teaspoons vanilla extract
$\frac{1}{2}$ teaspoon cinnamon
pinch of salt

tarte tatin

Whenever I have made this classic pudding in class it has met with audible gasps as the golden, caramelised apples appear as I turn it out. They look like jewels, all translucent and dripping with caramel. This is the secret to a truly fine Tarte Tatin – well caramelised apples. There are many methods documented, but our trials show that the best results are gained when the sugar is dissolved and caramelised in the butter first. If pastry making is not a priority, use a good quality, ready made puff or sweet short pastry.

for the pastry, place the flour, salt and butter in the food processor and blend until the mixture resembles breadcrumbs. Pulse in the egg yolk and enough cold water to bind. Tip the mixture out onto the bench and bring together quickly with your hands. Form into a disc, wrap and chill for 20 minutes.

Roll out into a $\frac{1}{2}$ cm ($\frac{1}{4}$") thick circle, slightly larger that the frying pan. Chill.

Preheat the oven to 220°C/450°F.

Melt the butter in a 24 cm (10") heavy, oven-proof pan. Add the sugar and stir to dissolve. Cook over a moderate heat until the sugar starts to caramelise.

Peel, core and halve the apples. Arrange them, cut-side up, on top of the butter and sugar.

Cook the apples gently until they are tender and golden.

Place the chilled pastry on top, tucking the edge down around the apples.

Bake until the pastry is cooked and nicely browned.

Remove from the oven, allow to rest for a minute, then invert the hot tart onto a platter. Any apples that stay behind can be placed back on the tart.

Serve warm with lightly whipped cream.

SERVES 8

PASTRY

250 g (9 oz) plain flour

1 teaspoon salt

125 g (4$\frac{1}{2}$ oz) unsalted butter, softened

1 egg yolk

cold water

APPLES

90 g (3$\frac{1}{2}$ oz) unsalted butter

100 g (4 oz) sugar

1 kg (2 lb 2 oz) cooking apples

elegant winter dining

Casual entertaining has taken over, but just now and again, on special occasions, it is fun to go 'elegant'. Bring out the silver and the fine china dinnerware, dress the table with candles and crystal and serve beautifully presented dishes with fine wines. It may sound like more work, but in fact it need not be. Plan an entrée and dessert that can be prepared ahead so only the main course will need last minute attention.

green soup

This is a very elegant cream soup with which to start a meal. In order to retain the fresh green of the vegetables, it's important to only just cook them and no more.

A soup like this needs to be seasoned perfectly. If you think it lacks something, try a small grating of fresh nutmeg or a squeeze of lemon juice. The mint, added at the end as a garnish, also adds an interesting and fresh flavour note.

melt the butter in a heavy-based stockpot over a medium heat and add the onion. Cook over a gentle heat until soft, then add the chicken stock and the peas and simmer until the peas are tender. Add the lettuce and cook until wilted.

Add the milk, transfer to a food processor or blender and purée until smooth.

Return to the saucepan and reheat. Season with salt and pepper.

Serve with a swirl of cream and a sprinkle of fresh, chopped mint.

SERVES 6

30 g (1 oz) unsalted butter

1 large onion, diced

750 ml (3 cups) chicken stock

1 kg (2 lb 2 oz) baby peas

1 cos lettuce, shredded

250 ml (1 cup) milk

sea salt and freshly ground pepper

90 ml (3 fl oz) cream

fresh mint

oyster soup with spinach and caviar

Greg Heffernan was one of the first local chefs to start teaching regularly at Epicurean way back in 1990. At that time he was executive chef at the renowned Huka Lodge where he was known for his elegant cuisine and use of local produce. Similar soups have been presented several times at different classes since, but Greg's is the one we keep going back to. It is perfectly okay to use frozen oysters, even for the garnish. Let them thaw slowly in a colander over a bowl to catch the juices. Don't wash them and they will taste just like fresh ones. A teaspoonful of caviar really finishes off this soup, but it is not essential.

melt the butter in a medium sized pot, then add the flour. Stir together, then cook over a gentle heat, stirring regularly, until the mixture just begins to colour. Add the cold fish stock, a little at a time, stirring to make a smooth sauce. Stir in all the champagne, then add the oysters and their juices.

Bring to a simmer, stirring often. Continue to simmer for 5 minutes. Add the milk, then bring back to a simmer. Transfer to a blender and purée. Pass through a sieve into a clean pot and set aside.

Toss the blanched spinach in butter over a steady heat and season to taste. Bring the soup back to the simmer and season to taste.

Whisk in all the whipped cream so that the soup is frothy on top.

Place a portion of hot buttered spinach in the centre of 10 flat soup plates, then top with 2 oysters and the caviar, if using. Ladle the soup around the spinach, garnish with chervil and serve hot.

SERVES 10

100 g (4 oz) unsalted butter
100 g (4 oz) plain flour
700 ml (1 1/4 pints) strong fish stock
250 ml (1 cup) methode champenoise
2 dozen frozen oysters and their juices
700 ml (1 1/4 pints) full cream milk
300 ml (1/2 pint) cream, softly whipped
sea salt and freshly ground pepper

GARNISH
2 bunches spinach leaves, washed, stalks removed and blanched
2 tablespoons butter
20 oysters
caviar (optional)
fresh chervil

salmon and wasabi ravioli with lime sauce

Donna Hay, the cookery editor at Marie Claire *magazine in Australia and author of, to date, three cookbooks of the same name, has taken the world by storm with her simple, innovative approach to good food. We thoroughly enjoyed her visit and look forward to the next one soon. This recipe is adapted from one in* Marie Claire Cooking. *Serve one or two ravioli as a first course, or more, with a salad, as a main dish.*

dice the salmon into small pieces. Mix the sour cream and ricotta together to make a firm paste and add the salmon, wasabi, basil and pepper.

Lay out the wonton wrappers and place spoonfuls of salmon mixture on top. Moisten the edges with water and cover with another wonton wrapper. Press firmly around the edges to expel any air and to seal well.

To make the sauce, combine the stock, lime leaves and cream and simmer gently until reduced by half.

Bring a large pot of water to a rolling boil. Add salt and cook the ravioli for 3–4 minutes. Drain, place in flat soup bowls and spoon over the sauce. Finish with a grind of black pepper.

SERVES 4–6

350 g (12$\frac{1}{2}$ oz) salmon fillet, skinned and pin bones removed (see glossary page 195)
$\frac{1}{3}$ cup sour cream
125 g (4$\frac{1}{2}$ oz) ricotta cheese
$\frac{1}{2}$ teaspoon wasabi paste
1 tablespoon chopped basil
freshly ground pepper
40 fresh wonton wrappers

S A U C E
1 cup fish stock
6 kaffir lime leaves, shredded, or the julienned zest of 2 lemons or limes
$\frac{3}{4}$ cup cream

braised duck with apples

Duck is still a treat for most of us, even though it is as readily available now as chicken. The breast of a duck is the meatiest part. When bought separately, there is no wastage – no heads, feet or bones to discard. Duck breasts usually sport a fairly impressive layer of fat under the skin. Much of this will render out during cooking, to be discarded, unless of course you decadently reserve it for frying potatoes.

season the duck breasts liberally with salt and pepper. Heat the oil in a heavy, deep pan and, when the oil is hot but not smoking, add the duck breasts and brown on the skin side only. Remove from the pan.

Reduce the heat a little, add the onion and cook until soft – about 5 minutes.

Return the duck to the pan, along with any juices. Add the wine, stock and apples. Cover, reduce the heat and simmer gently until the duck is tender, 10–15 minutes.

Remove the duck and rest, lightly covered. The sauce will have reduced while cooking but, if necessary, increase the heat and reduce further until syrupy.

Slice the duck breasts and arrange with the apple slices on a platter. Pour over the sauce and serve with this creamy potato gratin.

6 duck breasts

sea salt and freshly ground pepper

2 tablespoons extra virgin olive oil

2 onions, cut into eighths

500 ml (2 cups) dessert wine

500 ml (2 cups) duck or chicken stock

3 apples, peeled, cored and sliced into eighths

SERVES 6

creamy potato gratin

preheat the oven to 190°C/375°F.

Place the potatoes in a large saucepan and add the milk, water, garlic, salt and bayleaves. Bring to a boil, then reduce the heat and simmer until the potatoes are tender but not falling apart – about 10 minutes. Stir occasionally so they do not stick on the bottom. Using a slotted spoon, transfer half the potatoes to a large gratin dish. Sprinkle with the nutmeg, pepper, half the cream and half the cheese. Cover with the remaining potatoes and sprinkle again with nutmeg, pepper and the remaining cream and cheese.

Bake the gratin until crisp and golden on the top – about 1 hour.

1.5 kg (3½ lb) floury potatoes, such as Agria, peeled and sliced thinly

500 ml (2 cups) milk

500 ml (2 cups) water

3 cloves garlic, crushed

1 teaspoon salt

3 bayleaves

freshly ground nutmeg

freshly ground black pepper

250 ml (1 cup) cream

2 cups gruyere cheese, grated

roast pork scotch fillet with five-spice, orange and lemon zest and crunchy crackling

From Lauraine Jacobs' series 'Simply Delicious' comes this pork dish, redolent of spices and citrus. Lauraine adapted it from an original Ken Hom recipe and we think it is the most delicious way to prepare pork. The roasting method, with its cover of crackling, ensures the meat remains moist and succulent.

mix the five-spice powder, salt and pepper together and rub into the meat.

Crush the garlic with the skin on and sprinkle over the pork along with the lemon and orange zest and the sage. Leave for the flavours to permeate for at least 2 hours or overnight.

Heat the oven to 220°C/425°F.

Score the crackling with a sharp knife if this has not already been done. Place the pork in a roasting pan, and drape the crackling over the top to cover. Roast for 15 minutes, then reduce the oven temperature to 180°C/350°F. Continue roasting for 1 to 1½ hours until the juices run clear when the meat is pierced with the point of a small knife. Watch the crackling and remove it when it becomes crisp and crunchy, or, if it remains flat, place under a hot grill for a few minutes before serving.

Take the pork from the oven, place on a carving dish and cover with foil. To make a gravy, skim all but a little fat from the pan juices and deglaze the pan with a little white wine. Add the stock and the orange juice and bring to a simmer. Continue to simmer until the sauce is reduced by half. Strain to remove any bits, season with salt and pepper to taste and serve over the sliced pork, accompanied with roast kumara and fresh green beans.

SERVES 8–10

1 tablespoon five-spice powder
2 tablespoons sea salt
2 teaspoons freshly ground black pepper
2 kg (4½ lb) scotch fillet of pork, with crackling separate
5 cloves garlic
julienned zest of 1 lemon (about 1 tablespoon)
julienned zest of 1 orange
1 small handful fresh sage leaves
1 glass white wine
500 ml (2 cups) chicken stock
juice of 1 orange

caramelised risotto pudding with vanilla

Risotto does not have to be savoury, as you can see from this sweet version which I cooked in a risotto class last year. The English have always had rice pudding, only ever good if made with cream, so this recipe takes the best of both cuisines to produce a rich, creamy pudding flavoured with real vanilla and served with a crunchy, caramel lid. Use Italian Arborio or Carnaroli rice as an alternative to the Calasparra (Spanish paella rice).

combine the milk, sugar, rice and vanilla bean in a large saucepan and stir over a medium heat until the sugar has dissolved.

Cook over a low heat, stirring occasionally, until the liquid is absorbed and the rice is cooked through – approximately 20 minutes. The mixture should be thick and creamy. Remove from the heat.

Remove the vanilla bean and with a sharp knife slit the bean and gently scrape out the seeds.

Combine the egg yolks, cream and vanilla extract and stir into the rice with the vanilla bean seeds. Cook for 1 minute.

To serve, spoon the risotto pudding onto serving plates or into custard cups and sprinkle with caster sugar. Heat a brûlée iron over a high heat and hold over the sugar until it melts and caramelises. Alternatively use a kitchen torch.

SERVES 8

1 litre milk
150 g (5$\frac{1}{2}$ oz) caster sugar
300 g (11 oz) Calasparra rice
1 vanilla bean
2 egg yolks
$\frac{1}{2}$ cup (125 ml) cream
$\frac{1}{2}$ teaspoon vanilla extract
extra caster sugar

hot chocolate puddings

The Paul Bocuse restaurant in Melbourne is no more, but its founding chef Philippe Mouchel has stayed on, much to everyone's delight, at his new restaurant, Langton's.

This pudding was a spectacular end to a menu Philippe presented at Epicurean. Make sure you use the finest Callebaut or Valrhona chocolate and bring the puddings out of the oven when the centre is still liquid. When cut, the rich, creamy centre should flow out onto the plate.

butter and flour 8–10 125 ml (4 oz) moulds. Preheat the oven to 200°C/400°F.

Break the chocolate into small pieces and melt in a bowl over a pot of simmering water.

Beat in the butter and then the sugar. Stir through the flour until well combined. Add the eggs one by one, beating well after each addition.

Fill each mould $^3/_4$ full and place them on an oven-proof tray. Bake 9–10 minutes until risen and just starting to crack on top.

Remove from the oven and turn out onto plates. Serve with whipped cream and a few berries to garnish.

SERVES 8–10

110 g ($3^3/_4$ oz) good quality dark or bitter chocolate
115 g (4 oz) unsalted butter, softened
185 g ($6^1/_2$ oz) caster sugar
$^1/_2$ cup plain flour
4 eggs
whipped cream and berries

spur of the moment

This chapter is designed for spur of the moment entertaining, those times when having to prepare a meal for others is the last thing on your mind. If you keep a few basics in the pantry then there will always be something you can 'whip up', but this is not the time for formal, elegant food. Put it on a platter in the middle of the table. Meat cuts for fast cooking are inevitably the premium ones: chicken breast, pork or beef fillet and lamb cutlets.

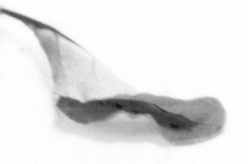

cellophane noodle salad

This dish, taught by Meera Freeman when she visited our school a few years ago, is redolent of all the flavours so often found in Southeast Asian food. Many of the Asian noodles are easy to use. Just boil the kettle and pour the water on. For busy people this is a wonderful thing! Dried, fried shrimp are bought ready to use and once opened the packet keeps forever in an airtight jar.

soak the noodles in hot water until tender and drain well (2–5 minutes). Cut them into short lengths with a pair of scissors to make them easier to serve.

Cook the chicken or pork thoroughly in a frying pan with the water, breaking up any lumps with a fork.

In a bowl, combine the lime juice, fish sauce and sugar and stir until the sugar is dissolved. Add this sauce to the pan with the meat, then add the noodles. Mix well, adding the shallot, ginger, celery, mushrooms, pickled garlic and coriander leaves. Season with the ground chilli to taste, then stir in the peanuts and shrimp.

Place on a serving dish and garnish with extra coriander leaves.

SERVES 6–8

150 g (5–6 oz) cellophane noodles (see glossary)
230 g (8 oz) minced raw chicken breast or minced pork
1 tablespoon water
2 tablespoons lime juice
2 tablespoons fish sauce
1 teaspoon palm sugar
1 tablespoon chopped shallot
1 tablespoon finely shredded ginger
1 tablespoon finely sliced celery
3 dried mushrooms, reconstituted in water and cut into pieces
1 pickled garlic bulb, finely sliced
1 tablespoon coriander leaves and extra to garnish
1 teaspoon ground dried chilli
1 tablespoon coarsely chopped roasted peanuts
1 tablespoon crisp fried dried shrimp

fresh salmon fishcakes with tartare sauce

This is a great way to make a little salmon go a long way. Even though it's the salmon that makes these fishcakes seem exotic, the secret is the roughly mashed potato. Homemade tartare sauce is a must and it can be made in a few minutes in a food processor.

preheat the oven to 200°C/400°F.

Place the salmon on a shallow baking tray and cover with foil. Cook for 6–8 minutes – it should be rare inside. Remove from the oven and allow to cool. Remove the skin and any bones and flake into a large bowl.

Mix in the potato and parsley and season well with the salt and pepper. Form into cakes – it will make approximately 12 cakes measuring 5 cm (2") in diameter. Chill the fishcakes until firm.

To make the tartare sauce, place the egg, mustard, lemon juice and tabasco in the bowl of a food processor and process together. Add the oil slowly in a thin, steady stream until the mixture forms an emulsion. Stir in the gherkins, parsley, shallot and capers and season with salt and pepper. Makes 1 cup.

Dip the salmon cakes into the beaten egg, then the breadcrumbs, making sure they are well coated.

Heat equal quantities of oil and butter until bubbling and cook the fishcakes until golden on each side. Serve with tartare sauce, lemon wedges and a crisp salad.

SERVES 4

500 g (1 lb) piece salmon fillet, skin on
300 g (11 oz) cooked potatoes, mashed roughly with a fork
1 tablespoon chopped flatleaf parsley
sea salt and freshly ground pepper
1–2 large eggs, beaten
1 cup breadcrumbs
butter
vegetable oil

TARTARE SAUCE
2 egg yolks or 1 whole egg
1 teaspoon Dijon mustard
2 tablespoons lemon juice
dash of tabasco
1 cup (250 ml) vegetable oil
$\frac{1}{4}$ cup finely chopped gherkins
$\frac{1}{4}$ cup chopped flatleaf parsley
1 shallot, finely chopped
2 tablespoons capers
sea salt and freshly ground pepper

chicken fried with garlic and pepper

These little spicy chicken morsels can be served with jasmine rice, but they also make a great small bite when served piled on a platter with a bowl of dipping sauce and toothpicks with which to dip. Sriracha sauce is the brand name for a smooth, hot chilli sauce.

in a mortar, pound the garlic, peppercorns and coriander root until a juicy paste is obtained.

Cut the chicken into bite sized pieces.

Heat a little oil in a pan and fry the paste until fragrant. Add the chicken pieces and fry until they have lost their raw pink look. Add the sugar and fish sauce and stir to combine well, continuing to cook until the chicken pieces are cooked through.

Garnish with the coriander leaves and serve with Sriracha sauce.

SERVES 4 WITH RICE

5 cloves garlic
1 tablespoon white peppercorns
1 tablespoon fresh coriander root, chopped
3 chicken breasts
vegetable oil for frying
1 teaspoon palm sugar
1 tablespoon fish sauce
coriander leaves
smooth chilli sauce such as Sriracha

broccoli with lemon and chilli

Broccoli is an everyday vegetable which very rarely gets any special treatment. Here is a simple way of making it more exciting.

combine the olive oil, chilli and anchovies in a small pan. Heat gently until the oil is warm and the anchovies 'melt'. Turn off the heat and set aside.

Trim the broccoli and separate into florets. Plunge into boiling salted water and cook until just tender. Drain and refresh under cold, running water. Transfer to a serving dish.

Whisk the lemon juice into the oil mixture and pour over the broccoli. Toss and season to taste with salt and pepper.

SERVES 4–6

$\frac{1}{4}$ cup (4 tablespoons) extra virgin olive oil
1 small fresh red chilli, finely chopped
3 anchovy fillets
750 g (1$\frac{3}{4}$ lb) broccoli
juice $\frac{1}{2}$ lemon
sea salt and freshly ground pepper

baked fish with almonds, onions and toasted breadcrumbs

I cooked this dish in a class series called 'What to Have for Dinner', so it's appropriate that I should include it in this chapter. Use any firm fleshed fish, but do ensure that it is only just cooked, even still a little rare. Fish cooked this way is so much more succulent.

preheat the oven to 180°C/350°F.

Spread the almonds on a baking sheet and toast until pale gold and fragrant. Allow to cool, then coarsely chop and combine with the toasted breadcrumbs.

Melt the butter in an oven-proof pan with deep sides. Add the onion and cook over a low heat until soft. Add the sage and lemon zest and season with salt and pepper. Set aside.

Raise the oven temperature to 230°C/450°F. Place the fish on top of the onion mixture and season with salt and pepper. Top with the almond and breadcrumb mixture.

Bake until the fish is just cooked through – 10–12 minutes. Garnish with lemon wedges.

SERVES 6

$\frac{1}{2}$ **cup sliced almonds**
$\frac{1}{2}$ **cup toasted breadcrumbs**
6 tablespoons unsalted butter
4 medium onions, diced in 1 cm ($\frac{1}{2}$") pieces
2 tablespoons chopped fresh sage
2 tablespoons grated lemon zest
sea salt and freshly ground pepper
6 fish fillets, such as salmon, hapuku or kingfish
lemon wedges

dill and cumin crusted baked poussin on
wilted rocket

Peter Chichester cooked these poussins in class and then again, by special request, for our staff Christmas party dinner last year. The poussin (baby chicken) could be replaced with chicken pieces. A delightful garnish is a fresh grape leaf, blanched briefly in boiling water, refreshed, dried then rubbed with a little oil and allowed to crisp up in the oven for a few minutes. Place one on top of each bird, or sit the bird on top of one and serve the wilted rocket separately.

preheat the oven to 180°C/350°F.

Place the breadcrumbs on a baking tray and drizzle or spray with olive oil. Toss well to coat and bake until the crumbs are golden and crisp. Cool.

Mix all the crust ingredients, except the breadcrumbs, together and chop finely.

Add the breadcrumbs and mix. Set aside.

Increase the oven to 200°C/400°F.

Line a roasting pan with the smashed garlic cloves, rosemary sprigs and bayleaves.

Tuck the poussin wings underneath and tie the legs and parson's nose together. Brush each poussin liberally with Dijon mustard and roll in the herbed crust mixture. Place in the roasting pan and season with sea salt.

Roast for 20 minutes or until the juices run clear when the meat if pierced with the point of a small knife. Remove from the oven and rest, lightly covered, for at least 10 minutes.

Toss the rocket leaves in a frying pan with butter. Season to taste with salt and pepper.

Serve each poussin on a bed of wilted rocket leaves.

SERVES 6

CRUST

200 g (7 oz) fresh breadcrumbs
olive oil
100 g (4 oz) fresh dill
100 g (4 oz) flatleaf parsley
3 tablespoons toasted, ground cumin
  seeds
zest of 2 lemons
3 cloves garlic
1 teaspoon chilli flakes
2 tablespoons ground coriander

garlic cloves, smashed with the back
  of a knife
rosemary sprigs
fresh bayleaves
6 poussins
smooth Dijon mustard

rocket leaves
butter
sea salt and freshly ground pepper

caramelised pork fillets with bok choy and mushrooms

I often cook this for dinner, either with pork or using boned chicken thighs. Use a mixture of whatever mushrooms are available. I usually use buttons and a few shiitake although sometimes I'll buy a box of the wonderfully exotic mushroom medley which contains the shiitake along with phoenix, wood ear and honeycomb. I particularly like the fact that I only have to pour boiling water over the egg noodles – no big pots of water to boil.

preheat the oven to 200°C/400°F.

Combine ¼ cup of peanut oil with the soy sauce and honey, and rub into the pork. Heat 1 tablespoon olive oil in a heavy-based oven-proof skillet and brown the pork on all sides over a high heat.

Transfer to the oven and cook for about 15 minutes or until the meat is just cooked through and the juices run clear. Rest, loosely covered, in a warm place for 5 minutes.

Heat the stock, soy and oyster sauces together in a small pan or in the microwave. Heat 3 tablespoons of peanut oil in a large wok and cook the mushrooms, garlic and ginger over a high heat for 1 minute. Add the bok choy and spinach and stir over a medium heat until just wilted. Add the hot stock mixture to the wok and simmer for about 5 minutes until the bok choy is tender.

Add boiling water to the noodles in a bowl and stand for 5–10 minutes. Drain.

To serve, slice the pork. Divide the noodles among 6 shallow bowls. Spoon over the bok choy mixture, top with slices of pork and drizzle with pan juices.

SERVES 6

peanut or vegetable oil

2 tablespoons soy sauce

1 tablespoon honey

600 g (21 oz) pork fillets, trimmed of any sinew

1 cup (250 ml) chicken stock

1 tablespoon soy sauce

1 tablespoon oyster sauce

350 g (12 oz) mixed mushrooms, sliced

1 clove garlic, chopped

1 teaspoon chopped ginger

3 baby bok choy, quartered

1 bunch small spinach, trimmed and washed

100 g (4 oz) dried Chinese egg noodles

mu-shu pork

In talking to the many people who attend our classes I have concluded that there are few kitchens these days that do not possess a wok. The benefits of wok cooking are many, not least that it is fast. My wok has a flat base and a durable non-stick surface (I long ago gave up on traditional Chinese woks which rust so readily when not in use every day). It also has one long handle with a grip on the opposite side which I find far easier to use. This dish is a great one-bowl meal.

place the pork, soy sauce, rice wine, sugar, sesame oil and salt and pepper in a small bowl, toss and set aside.

Heat the peanut oil in a large wok over a high heat. Add the pork and toss until lightly coloured. Add the ginger, spring onions, cabbage, carrots, and mushrooms. Stirfry, tossing constantly until the pork is cooked through – 4–5 minutes.

Serve immediately with warm plum sauce, on rice, noodles or inside a warm flour tortilla, mountain bread or crepes.

SERVES 4

225 g (8 oz) pork fillet, sinew removed, cut into very thin strips
4 tablespoons soy sauce
2 tablespoons rice wine or dry sherry
2 teaspoons sugar
1 tablespoon toasted sesame oil
salt and freshly ground pepper
2 tablespoons peanut oil
$\frac{1}{4}$ cup thin slivers of fresh ginger
8 spring onions, cut into 5 cm (2") long julienne
$\frac{1}{2}$ Savoy cabbage, cored and sliced finely
2 carrots, peeled and cut into a fine julienne
10 shiitake mushrooms, finely sliced

grilled bratwurst and potato salad

Ray McVinnie has been teaching at Epicurean since 1991 and he is one of our most popular tutors. His food is inspired, it's accessible and it suits today's lifestyle. He is perhaps best known for his barbecue classes and as I say in the schedule – no sausages and chops here. Well here's an exception – bratwurst, the king of all sausages, especially when prepared this way. Choose small waxy potatoes, so they won't fall apart on the grill.

parboil the potatoes. Drain, dry them well and toss with the olive oil and garlic. Set aside.

Preheat a barbecue or ridged grill.

Combine the dressing ingredients and mix well. Season to taste with salt and pepper.

Grill the bratwurst until well browned and cooked through. Slice 3 cm (1¼") thick.

Grill the potatoes until crusty, golden and cooked through.

Combine the potatoes and sausage and pile onto a platter. Pour over the dressing and serve.

SERVES 4–5

10 small, red waxy potatoes, halved lengthways
1 cup extra virgin olive oil
4 cloves garlic, finely chopped
6 bratwurst sausages

DRESSING
200 ml (7 fl oz) extra virgin olive oil
5 tablespoons cider vinegar
½ cup capers, rinsed and drained
4 gherkins, sliced
1 red capsicum, roasted, peeled, seeded and chopped (page 196)
½ red onion, finely chopped
½ cup fresh dill, chopped
½ cup Italian parsley leaves, roughly chopped
sea salt and freshly ground pepper

lamb cutlets with artichokes and olives

Lauraine Jacobs, well known food writer and restaurant critic, has for the last few years conducted a series of classes for us called 'Simply Delicious'. Each class looks at dishes which can be achieved in a short time. Lamb cutlets are a little like chicken breasts – quick to cook and easy to dress up into something special. This is one of those dishes.

take a large heavy-based pan and heat 3 tablespoons of olive oil. Over a medium heat cook the lamb cutlets briefly on each side until they are well coloured. Remove and keep to the side, covered in foil.

Add the onion, parsley and garlic to the pan and cook slowly for 5 minutes until soft and melting. Turn the heat up, add the wine and cook quickly to reduce by half. Add the artichokes, cut in half or sliced, the olives and the lemon juice.

Bring this to a simmer, and season with salt and pepper to taste. Return the lamb cutlets to the pan and cook at simmering point for 3–4 minutes until the lamb is cooked but still pink in the centre.

SERVES 6

extra virgin olive oil
18 baby lamb cutlets
1 small onion, finely chopped
3 tablespoons Italian parsley
2 cloves garlic, crushed
1 cup (250 ml) dry white wine
12 small artichokes (fresh or preserved in oil)
1 cup tiny Niçoise or Taggiasche olives
juice of 1 lemon
sea salt and freshly ground pepper

chilled lemon cream

In Everyday Epicurean *I featured several dishes from my week spent in Italy in 1997 with Maggie Beer and Stephanie Alexander. This dessert is another of the wonderful memories I have of that week, even two years later. It's very pretty, especially decorated with glazed lemon slices. Prepare these whenever you have some free time. They store in the fridge for weeks and can be used to garnish cakes and other desserts.*

sprinkle the broken biscuits with the wine.

Whisk the egg yolks with the caster sugar until pale and thick and mix in the lemon zest.

In another bowl, beat the egg whites until stiff but not dry. With a large metal spoon gently fold a $\frac{1}{4}$ of the whites into the yolk mixture, then very carefully fold in the remaining whites.

Whip the cream and fold it into the egg mixture with the soaked biscuits.

Spoon the mixture into individual moulds and freeze for 1 hour (the mixture is not meant to become solid). Decorate with a glazed lemon slice and dust with icing sugar just before serving.

3 sponge finger (savoiardi) biscuits, broken into pieces
$\frac{1}{4}$ cup (4 tablespoons) sweet wine, Vin Santo or Marsala
3 eggs, separated
75 g ($2\frac{3}{4}$ oz) caster sugar
grated zest of 3 lemons
$1\frac{1}{2}$ cups (375 ml) cream
glazed lemon slices

glazed lemon slices

slice the lemons very thinly (a Benriner mandolin does the job easily) and remove any pips.

Cover with boiling water and allow to stand for 3 hours.

Combine the sugar and water and bring to the boil, stirring to dissolve the sugar. Simmer for 5 minutes then add the drained lemon slices. Simmer very gently for about 50–60 minutes until the skins of the lemons are translucent and the liquid has reduced to a syrup.

Cool and store in the fridge.

8 Meyer lemons
500 g (1 lb) sugar
2 cups (500 ml) water

little caramel puddings

These simple puddings make a surprisingly elegant dessert. Just place each one on a plate to serve and have a bowl of whipped cream on the table.

preheat the oven to 180°C/350°F.

Combine the caramel ingredients and divide evenly between 6 x 200 ml (7 fl oz) ramekins.

Beat the butter and sugar together in a bowl until creamy. Add the eggs, one at a time, beating well. Add the vanilla, then gently mix through the flour and then the milk.

Spoon into the prepared ramekins and bake for approximately 20 minutes or until golden.

Serve warm with softly whipped cream.

MAKES 6

CARAMEL

397 g (7 oz) tin condensed milk

30 g (1 oz) unsalted butter, melted

4 tablespoons golden syrup

PUDDING

90 g (3$\frac{1}{2}$ oz) unsalted butter

$\frac{3}{4}$ cup sugar

2 eggs

1 teaspoon vanilla extract

$\frac{3}{4}$ cup self-raising flour

$\frac{1}{3}$ cup milk

roasted fruits with verjuice and almonds

Fruit always features after a meal in North Africa. It may be a plate of fresh fruits or a dish of poached fruits, flavoured with orange flower or rose water, honey, almond or spices like cardamom, cinnamon and clove. Sometimes I prepare this recipe with just one fruit, but at other times, depending what is available, I use a mixture. White wine may be used as a substitute for verjuice (see page 197).

preheat the oven to 200°C/400°F.

Cut the fruit into quarters and remove the pits and seeds.

Combine the honey, sugar, verjuice and spices in a baking dish . Add the fruit and toss well to coat.

Bake until the fruit is tender, 15–20 minutes, turning once or twice. Remove from the oven and cool.

Lower the oven temperature to 180°C/350°F.

Toss the almonds and sugar together, add the egg white and mix well.

Spread the mixture onto a lined or greased baking sheet and bake, turning every 5 minutes, until golden and caramelised.

Transfer the fruit to a pretty serving plate and sprinkle with the almonds just before serving.

SERVES 4–6

selection of fresh seasonal fruit –
  plums, peaches, nectarines, pears,
  figs
2 tablespoons honey
2 tablespoons light brown sugar
2 tablespoons verjuice
whole spices – cinnamon stick, star
  anise, vanilla bean

³/₄ cup sliced almonds
¹/₄ cup sugar
1 large egg white

glossary

baking blind This term refers to the baking of an unfilled pastry case. Once the pastry has been rolled out and fitted into the tin, line it with a sheet of baking paper, fitting it into the edges of the tart. To prevent the pastry from collapsing during baking, fill with ceramic or metal baking beans and place in a hot, 200°C/400°F, oven to bake. After about 20 minutes remove the beans and paper and return to the oven until the pastry is cooked.

blanch Used to par cook and set the colour of vegetables. Plunge the vegetables into boiling water, bring back to the boil and then remove and refresh under cold water. This same method is also used to loosen the skins on tomatoes, onions and almonds before peeling.

cellophane noodles Very thin, transparent Chinese noodles made from mung beans.

Chinese greens There are many different Chinese greens. The most common are bok choy (also known as pak choy), choy sum and gai larn (Chinese broccoli). All are used in soups or stirfries or steamed on their own as a vegetable.

couscous A form of pasta used in North African cuisine – coarsely ground semolina is mixed to a dough with water and salt and rolled into tiny balls that are steamed. Today the 'instant' variety is widely used.

ferron rice Normally it is necessary to stir risotto constantly during cooking to release the starch. Ferron rice (Vialone Nano or Carnaroli), organically grown and traditionally milled, has more starch than other rices, making stirring unnecessary. Use twice the amount of liquid to rice.

fish sauce (nuoc ma'm or nam pla) I call it the salt of Southeast Asia. It is a clear, amber liquid derived from fermented fish. Used as a flavouring and in dipping sauces. Keeps indefinitely. It tastes much better than it smells.

flour The cakes featured throughout this book call for plain flour. This is a soft flour and is also called standard or pure flour. High grade flour describes strong flour suitable for breadmaking.

kecap manis A thick, sweet soy sauce.

lemongrass A fibrous grass, valued for its flavour. Use only the bulbous root end and the core.

mayonnaise

> *3 egg yolks*
> *1 tablespoon lemon juice or white wine vinegar*
> *150 ml extra virgin olive oil*
> *sea salt and freshly ground pepper*
> *150 ml vegetable oil*
> *white pepper or Tabasco sauce*

Place the egg yolks and lemon juice or vinegar in the bowl of a food processor and blend until smooth. Very gradually add the olive oil in a thin stream with the food processor turned on. When the mixture has amalgamated, the rest of the olive oil can be added in a steady stream.

Taste for acidity and adjust with drops of lemon juice, salt and pepper. If you prepare the mayonnaise ahead of time, store in the refrigerator with plastic wrap pressed onto the surface to prevent a skin forming.

mirin A type of rice wine or 'sweet sake' with added sugar, used in cooking.

nori Paper-thin sheets of seaweed used in sushi-making. Buy the packets of toasted nori.

Parmesan cheese Throughout this book when I refer to Parmesan I do not mean the canisters of granules of the same name. I urge you to look for Italian Parmigiano Reggiano, the finest of Parmesan cheeses from the Italian region of Parma, and buy a small wedge, with the rind on. Store it, wrapped in muslin, in a plastic container with a lid, in the fridge. Grate or shave the cheese as you need it or serve it with fresh pears instead of dessert. Stored correctly, it will last for months. A good alternative is grana padano, a similar cheese made in other regions of Italy.

palm sugar The nectar of palm trees is boiled and evaporated then moulded into cakes of various shapes. The darker sugar has a richer, more caramelised flavour. Chop or grate before using. As an alternative use soft brown sugar.

pate sucrée – sweet short pastry

  170 g (6 oz) plain flour
  pinch of salt
  85 g (3 oz) caster sugar
  85 g (3 oz) unsalted butter, diced and chilled
  3 egg yolks, lightly beaten
  2 drops vanilla extract

Place the flour, salt and sugar in the bowl of a food processor and pulse briefly. Drop in the butter and process until the mixture resembles breadcrumbs.

Using the pulse button, pour in the egg yolks and vanilla and blend until just combined. Tip the mixture out onto the bench and bring together quickly by hand. Form into a flat disc, wrap in plastic film and refrigerate for at least 30 minutes before rolling.

pin bones in salmon A side of salmon has a row of fine bones running almost along its entire length. To remove them, run your finger down the flesh against the grain and the bones will pop up. Use tweezers to extract the bones, being careful to pull them out with the grain.

polenta A grainy flour made from yellow or white corn. Can be cooked like a porridge or allowed to set so it can be sliced and grilled. The Italians use only water or a little milk when cooking polenta, but I find it has more flavour when cooked in a light chicken or vegetable stock.

creamy polenta

  2 litres (8 cups) chicken stock
  1 cup cream
  2 teaspoons crushed garlic
  1/2 cup Parmesan cheese, freshly grated
  3/4 cup fine polenta
  1 cup semolina
  salt and freshly ground black pepper

Place the chicken stock, cream and garlic into a large pot and heat until boiling. Add the grated Parmesan and slowly pour in the polenta and semolina, whisking to combine. Cook over a low temperature for 20 minutes. Season well with salt and pepper.

grilled polenta

  1 1/2 litres light chicken stock
  300 g (11 oz) instant polenta
  50 g (3 tablespoons) butter
  50 g (3 tablespoons) freshly grated Parmesan cheese
  sea salt and freshly ground pepper
  olive oil

Bring the stock to the boil. Slowly pour the polenta into the boiling stock, whisking constantly. Continue stirring with a wooden spoon for 5–10 minutes.

Stir in the butter and Parmesan cheese, season well and tip out onto a greased tray. Spread out to approximately 5 mm (2") thick.

Allow to cool then cut into wedges. Brush with olive oil and grill or fry until golden.

potatoes For salads, waxy potatoes are best. These include Jersey Benne, Desiree, Nadine and Draga. Floury potatoes are suitable for mashing and roasting. Floury varieties include Agria, Red Rascal, Karaka and Rua.

preserved lemons These lemons are used widely in Middle Eastern cookery. The following method is very easy. Store the jars in a dark, cool place and they will last at least a year. When you come to use them, remove the flesh and discard. Chop or slice the rind finely.

  coarse sea salt
  lemons, scrubbed and cut into quarters
  1 bay leaf
  a few cloves
  1 cinnamon stick
  extra lemon juice or boiling water

Choose a large, wide-mouthed jar and sterilise it. Sprinkle a little salt in the base. Place the lemons in a bowl with plenty of salt and massage them well until the juice starts to run. Pack them into the jar, along with the spices. Tip in the lemon juice and salt and cover with extra lemon juice or boiling water. Remove the salt from the neck of the jar with a clean cloth dipped in boiling water, and seal. Allow the lemons to pickle for at least 4 weeks before using.

rice noodles Different varieties exist, fresh and dried. Rice stick noodles – soak for 30 seconds in cold water; boil for 4–7 minutes. Rice vermicelli – deep-fry in hot oil to make nests or soak for 2 minutes in boiling water before using. Rinse fresh noodles in warm water and add to stirfries or soups.

rice vinegar A Chinese vinegar that can be red, black or white. The white is most commonly used as a flavouring agent in soups and in sweet and sour dishes. Sometimes referred to as rice wine vinegar.

roasted capsicum Red, green, yellow, orange and black – capsicums come in myriad colours, but all essentially taste the same. Roasting or grilling sweetens the flesh and removes the thin, bitter skin, and can also add a delicious barbecue flavour. Resist the temptation to peel the capsicum under running water. This will wash away all the flavour. Simply wash your hands as you peel.

- To roast: Place the capsicums on a baking tray in a hot (200°C/400°F) oven and roast until the skin is black and blistered. Remove and cover with tinfoil or a clean teatowel. When cool enough to handle peel off the skin.
- To grill or barbecue: Hold the capsicum over the flame of a gas burner or place on the open grill of a barbecue. When the skin is charred and blistered, remove and follow the steps described above.

roasted garlic Roasting garlic makes it sweet rather than pungent. Take a whole head of garlic and remove any excess papery skin. Slice the top off the entire head. Rub the garlic with olive oil and bake in a moderate (180°C/350°F) oven for about 45 minutes, until it is soft. Squeeze the garlic from the skins.

stocks Stock is the most important liquid base used in the preparation of many dishes, such as soups, sauces, casseroles etc. These days it is possible to buy commercial stocks. Most have added salt so it is advisable to dilute them well before use. Good, natural stocks are inexpensive to prepare, and if made correctly will greatly enhance the finished dish.

beef stock

> $1\frac{1}{2}$ *kg (3$\frac{1}{2}$ lb) beef bones*
> *5 litres (8$\frac{3}{4}$ pints) cold water*
> *100 g (4 oz) each carrot, onion, celery and leeks*
> *1 bouquet garni – a bayleaf, parsley stalks and sprig of thyme*
> *about 12 peppercorns*

OPTIONAL
> *100 g (4 oz) tomatoes*
> *50 g (1$\frac{3}{4}$ oz) mushroom trimmings*

- Have the bones chopped small. Remove any fat.
- Place the bones in a roasting dish and roast at 200°C/400°F until the bones have become an even brown colour.
- Drain off fat and place the bones in a large stockpot.
- Cover with the cold water and bring to the boil. Skim well.
- Wash, trim and cut the carrots, onions, leeks and celery roughly.
- Fry vegetables in a little hot oil or butter until golden brown.
- Drain and add vegetables, bouquet garni and peppercorns to the stockpot.
- Simmer gently for approximately 6 hours skimming where necessary.
- Strain, cool rapidly and store in the refrigerator until required.
- To reduce to a glace – remove any solidified fat. Bring to the boil and simmer gently until the stock has reduced by three-quarters. Cool, pour into ice cube trays and freeze. Each cube will reconstitute to approximately 1 cup of stock.

chicken stock This is a general purpose stock which is used in recipes where a compatible flavour and colour is not essential.

> $1\frac{1}{2}$ *kg (3$\frac{1}{2}$ lb) chicken bones*
> *5 litres (8$\frac{3}{4}$ pints) cold water*
> *100 g (4 oz) each carrot, onion, celery and leeks*
> *1 bouquet garni – a bayleaf, parsley stalks and sprig of thyme*
> *about 12 peppercorns*

- Have the bones chopped small. Remove any fat.
- Place the bones in a stockpot, cover with water, bring to the boil and skim well. (You can strain this water off instead of skimming and replenish with the fresh water.)
- Peel the carrots and onions. Wash and drain the celery and leeks.
- Add the vegetables, bouquet garni and peppercorns to the stockpot.
- Simmer gently for approximately 6 hours, skimming where necessary.
- Strain, cool rapidly and keep in the refrigerator for further use.

fish stock Cook fish stock for only 20 minutes. After that the bones will start to break down and impart a bitter flavour.

> **1 onion**
> **30 g (1 oz) butter**
> **$\frac{1}{2}$ bayleaf**
> **4-6 peppercorns**
> **few stalks parsley**
> **juice one lemon**
> **1 kg (2 lb) fresh fish bones (well washed)**
> **2$\frac{1}{2}$ litres (4$\frac{1}{2}$ pints) cold water**

- Peel and slice the onion.
- Heat the butter in a deep saucepan and add the onion, bayleaf, peppercorns, parsley, lemon juice and fish bones.
- Cover and stew lightly for 5 minutes, without colouring.
- Add the cold water and bring to the boil, skim and simmer gently for 20 minutes.
- Strain immediately and refrigerate.

tamari A fine Japanese soy sauce which should be made only from soy beans and rice, not wheat. It has a rich colour and flavour.

toasting and grinding spices Buy spices in small quantities. Toasting greatly enhances the flavour of whole spices. Heat a heavy based pan and toss the spice over a medium heat until fragrant, but not too dark. Cool a little and grind, either in an electric grinder (a coffee grinder used only for spices does a good job) or by hand in a mortar and pestle.

verjuice In the 14th and 15th centuries French cooks used this juice made from unripe grapes. It has the tartness of lemon and the acidity of vinegar but without the harshness of either. Use it to deglaze pans, make vinaigrettes, or poach fruit in a syrup made from equal parts verjuice and sugar. Read Maggie Beer's books for many ideas. Maggie makes it, the Epicurean imports it. Use white wine vinegar as an alternative in vinaigrettes or white wine for sauces or sweet applications.

wasabi A pale green paste made from the very hot root of a native Japanese plant. Available ready made in a tube or as a powder, which is then mixed with water.

wonton wrappers Small squares of pastry used for wontons or spring rolls. Available fresh or frozen they also come in various sizes and thicknesses. Can be used instead of pasta for ravioli.

STANDARD MEASUREMENTS

I can't stress enough the importance of accurate measuring tools, especially for baking. Ideally every kitchen should be equipped with a set of scales, measuring spoons and cups (for dry ingredients) and a measuring jug for liquids.

Always follow one set of measures in a recipe. Do not mix them up.

Teaspoon, tablespoon and cup measures are level, not heaped, unless otherwise indicated.

The measurements in this book are based on the following and in some cases have been rounded to the nearest ounce in the conversion from metric.

1 teaspoon	=	5 ml
1 tablespoon	=	15 ml/$\frac{1}{2}$ fl oz (Australia = 20 ml)
1 oz/fl oz	=	28.35 g/ml
1 UK pint	=	20 fl oz/567 ml
1 US pint	=	16 fl oz
1 litre	=	35 fl oz (1 US quart)
1 cup	=	250 ml

eggs Unless large eggs are specified, size 6 eggs have been used. This is a standard size egg. Large eggs are size 7.

ALTERNATIVE NAMES

baking paper	parchment paper/silicone paper
cannellini beans	white kidney beans
capsicum	bell pepper/sweet pepper
coriander	cilantro
courgettes	zucchini
eggplant	aubergine
golden syrup	dark corn syrup
icing sugar	confectioners sugar
plain flour	standard/pure flour
polenta	coarse cornmeal
prawn	jumbo shrimp
rocket	rocquette/arugula
spring onions	green onions

index